Cambridge Elements ≡

Elements in Music and Musicians 1750–1850
edited by
Simon P. Keefe
University of Sheffield

THE AGE OF MUSICAL ARRANGEMENTS IN EUROPE, 1780–1830

Nancy November
The University of Auckland

CAMBRIDGE
UNIVERSITY PRESS

Shaftesbury Road, Cambridge CB2 8EA, United Kingdom

One Liberty Plaza, 20th Floor, New York, NY 10006, USA

477 Williamstown Road, Port Melbourne, VIC 3207, Australia

314–321, 3rd Floor, Plot 3, Splendor Forum, Jasola District Centre, New Delhi – 110025, India

103 Penang Road, #05–06/07, Visioncrest Commercial, Singapore 238467

Cambridge University Press is part of Cambridge University Press & Assessment, a department of the University of Cambridge.

We share the University's mission to contribute to society through the pursuit of education, learning and research at the highest international levels of excellence.

www.cambridge.org
Information on this title: www.cambridge.org/9781108931601

DOI: 10.1017/9781108942584

First published 2023

A catalogue record for this publication is available from the British Library.

ISBN 978-1-108-93160-1 Paperback
ISSN 2732-558X (online)
ISSN 2732-5571 (print)

The Age of Musical Arrangements in Europe, 1780–1830

Elements in Music and Musicians 1750–1850

DOI: 10.1017/9781108942584
First published online: August 2023

Nancy November
The University of Auckland

Author for correspondence: Nancy November, n.november@auckland.ac.nz

Abstract: This Element considers the art and culture of arranging music in Europe in the period 1780–1830, using Haydn's London symphonies and Mozart's operas as its principal examples. The degree to which musical arrangements shaped the social, musical, and ideological landscape in this era deserves further attention. The Element focuses on Vienna, and an important era in the culture of arrangements, in which arrangements were widely and variously cultivated, and canon formation and the conception of musical works underwent crucial development. Piano transcriptions (for two hands, four hands, and two pianos) became ever more prominent, completely taking over the field after 1850.

This Element also has a video abstract: www.cambridge.org/Music and Musicians 1750–1850_Nancy November_abstract

Keywords: arrangements, chamber music, domestic music-making, Haydn, Mozart, opera, symphony

ISBNs: 9781108931601 (PB), 9781108942584 (OC)
ISSNs: 2732-558X (online), 2732-5571 (print)

Contents

To arrange, arranged: is used when a piece of music is set up for other instruments or for fewer voices than the score contains. For example, one has entire operas arranged for wind instruments only, or as quartets.[1]

1 The Idea of Arrangement

Writing on 'arrangement' in his 1802 *Musicalisches Lexikon*, Heinrich Christoph Koch mentions as his example the most common type of musical arrangement in his time: translations of public or large-scale works for smaller-scale ensembles. The practice of arranging works like operas, symphonies, and concertos for chamber ensemble was widespread around 1800. But chamber works were also 'scaled up', string quartets, for example, being arranged as symphonies; or scaled down, for instance songs being rearranged for solo piano. Koch notes the preferred media for arrangement in his era: wind ensembles and (string) quartets. Fifty years after Koch the priorities had changed and the piano was firmly established as the preferred medium for arrangement. Piano transcriptions – for two hands, four hands, and two pianos – became more and more prominent in the nineteenth century, completely taking over the field after 1850, by which time other varieties of arrangement had dwindled in popularity. This Element considers the culture of musical arrangements in Europe circa 1780–1830, using Haydn's later symphonies and Mozart operas as its principal musical focal points. This was a crucial era for arrangements, when they were most widely and variously cultivated. The final section looks briefly beyond these dates to consider how this culture changed, and persisted, in the later nineteenth century.

Short articles by Christopher Hogwood and Warwick Lister reveal aspects of the art and culture of musical arrangement in London in the late eighteenth century, dealing respectively with works by Haydn and Mozart;[2] and there are several studies of arrangements of Beethoven's symphonies.[3] But in the scholarship on arrangements, the emphasis has been on the later nineteenth century,

---

[1] Heinrich Christoph Koch, *Musikalisches Lexikon* (Frankfurt: August der Jüngere, 1802), p. 166 (all translations are mine unless otherwise noted).

[2] Christopher Hogwood, 'In Praise of Arrangements: The "Symphony Quintetto"', in Otto Biba and David Wyn Jones (eds.), *Studies in Music History Presented to H. C. Robbins Landon on His Seventieth Birthday* (London: Thames and Hudson, 1996), pp. 82–104; Warwick Lister, 'Dragonetti, Viotti and Those Superb Sextets of Mozart', *The Musical Times* 157/1937 (2016), pp. 3–5.

[3] Hans Grüß, 'Bearbeitung – Arrangement – Instrumentation als Form der Aneignung musikalischer Werke von Beethoven und Schubert', in Andreas Michel (ed.), *Ansichtssachen: Notate, Aufsätze, Collagen* (Altenburg: Kamprad, 1999), pp. 31–46; Michael Ladenburger, 'Aus der Not eine Tugend? Beethovens Symphonien in Übertragungen für kleinere Besetzungen', in Bernhard R. Appel (ed.), *Von der Ersten bis zur Neunten: Beethovens Symphonien im Konzert und im Museum* (Bonn: Beethoven-Haus, 2008), pp. 17–29.

and the focus on piano transcriptions, neglecting the broad array of genres for arrangement that were popular in the early nineteenth century.[4] Thus we have missed the considerable cultural, musical, and historical insight to be gained from studying and performing arrangements – especially the diverse arrangements that flourished in the time of Haydn and Mozart. The shaping effect of musical arrangements on the social, musical, and ideological landscape in that era deserves far more attention than it has thus far received. I have addressed this gap in recent publications, especially *Beethoven Symphonies Arranged for the Chamber* (2021) and *Cultivating String Quartets in Beethoven's Vienna* (2017); and in an essay on arrangements of the London symphonies.[5] This Element extends my previous work.

Arrangements of Haydn's symphonies are ideal to explore for the period 1780–1830 because they were many and varied (see Section 3). They show the shifts in the roles and types of arrangements made and performed during a crucial time in canon formation and the development of concert life. But arrangements of these symphonies need to be set in the context of the diverse genres that were considered suitable for arrangement (discussed in Section 2). There was an especially voracious appetite for arranging opera, both excerpts and entire works, as observed by Koch. So arrangements of Mozart's later operas form another focal point for discussion (Section 4), which shows how arrangements worked slightly differently in the case of opera.

Vienna receives much attention in this book, reflecting the number and variety of arrangements produced there, for various reasons: the rise of music publishing, the slow birth of concert life, and, not least, the desires of amateurs. Arrangements satisfied their want and need to re-hear and re-experience Viennese public music in their homes, including the works of Haydn, Mozart, Beethoven, and many others. Contemporary audiences found that arrangements

---

[4] Thomas Christensen, 'Four-Hand Piano Transcription and Geographies of Nineteenth-Century Musical Reception', *Journal of the American Musicological Society* 52/2 (1999), pp. 255–98; Kara Lynn van Dine, 'Musical Arrangements and Questions of Genre: A Study of Liszt's Interpretive Approaches' (PhD dissertation, University of North Texas, 2010); Zsuzsanna Domokos, '"Orchestration des Pianofortes": Beethovens Symphonien in Transkriptionen von Franz Liszt und seinen Vorgängern', in *Studia Musicologica Academiae Scientiarum Hungaricae* 37/2–5 (1996), pp. 227–318; Jonathan Kregor, *Liszt as Transcriber* (New York: Cambridge University Press, 2010); Mark Kroll, 'On a Pedestal and under the Microscope: The Arrangements of Beethoven Symphonies by Liszt and Hummel', in Markéta Štefková (ed.), *Franz Liszt und seine Bedeutung in der europäischen Musikkultur* (Bratislava: Ustav hudonej Vedy SAV, 2012), pp. 123–44.

[5] See my *Beethoven's Symphonies Arranged for the Chamber* (Cambridge: Cambridge University Press, 2021); *Cultivating String Quartets in Beethoven's Vienna* (Woodbridge: Boydell, 2017); and 'Domesticating Late Haydn: Arrangements of the London Symphonies and the Early Nineteenth-Century Performing Canon', in Federico Gon (ed.), *Haydn's Last Creative Period (1781–1801)* (Turnhout: Brepols, 2021), pp. 61–78.

helped them understand and enjoy often complex symphonies. People wanted to relive the 'surprise' in the Andante of Haydn's Symphony No. 94, for example, in the privacy and comfort of the home. And listeners also wanted to delve into the complexities of these composers' multilayered works, which went by all too fast on first listening.

Arrangement also flourished with the boom in the music publishing industry (see Section 2). This pertains especially to Vienna around 1800, but this Element also considers how practices, cultures, and markets differed between locations, including London in particular. However, I keep people, rather than places, in the foreground: the publishers, composers, performers, and listeners who used and promoted arrangements to their various ends. Catering to the end user, most arrangements were published in individual parts rather than scores during this era: the emphasis was on pragmatism and playability. But the reader can also refer to several arrangements of music from the era that are available in recent score and performing editions.[6] In these editions, Mozart has been a focus, and more recently Beethoven, but the popularity around 1800 of arrangements of Haydn's symphonies is not reflected in recent publications.

These modern editions of late eighteenth- and early nineteenth-century arrangements represent a tiny fraction of a vast number, which we can see reflected in Johann Traeg's Viennese publishing catalogue (see Section 2), for example. A key reason for the paucity of modern editions is that twentieth- and twenty-first-century scholars still tend to deride these early arrangements as hastily produced, low-quality spin-offs for a popular market, which generally do not respect nor fully represent their originals.[7] This is a hangover from later nineteenth-century views. So, for example, in 1909 Hugo Botstiber was quick to denounce the publication of Haydn's 'Paris' Symphonies arranged as quartets in

---

[6] The most relevant here are: Mark Kroll (ed.), *Twelve Select Overtures, Arranged for Pianoforte, Flute, Violin and Violoncello by J. N. Hummel*, Recent Researches in the Music of the Nineteenth and Early Twentieth Centuries, vol. 35 (Middleton, WI: A-R Editions, 2003); Mark Kroll (ed.), *Mozart's 'Haffner' and 'Linz' Symphonies, Arranged for Pianoforte, Flute, Violin and Violoncello by J. N. Hummel*, Recent Researches in the Music of the Nineteenth and Early Twentieth Centuries, vol. 29 (Middleton, WI: A-R Editions, 2000); Nancy November (ed.), *Chamber Arrangements of Beethoven's Symphonies*, pt 2, *Wellington's Victory and Symphonies Nos. 7 and 8 Arranged for String Quintet*, Recent Researches in Nineteenth-Century Music, vol. 77 (Middleton, WI: A-R Editions, 2019); Nancy November (ed.), *Chamber Arrangements of Beethoven's Symphonies*, pt 1, *Symphonies Nos. 1, 3, and 5 Arranged for Quartet Ensembles*, Recent Researches in Nineteenth-Century Music, vol. 75 (Middleton, WI: A-R Editions, 2019); Nancy November (ed.), *Chamber Arrangements of Beethoven's Symphonies*, pt 3, *Symphonies Nos. 2, 4, and 6 Arranged for Large Ensembles*, Recent Researches in Nineteenth-Century Music, vol. 79 (Middleton, WI: A-R Editions, 2020); and Uwe Grodd (ed.), *Johann Nepomuk Hummel: Mozart's Six Grand Symphonies [for Flute, Violin, Cello and Piano]* (Wellington: Artaria Editions, 2015).

[7] Hogwood, 'In Praise of Arrangements', p. 83.

1787, and would not entertain the idea that Haydn had arranged them himself: 'From whom the arrangements came is not known. Certainly not Haydn himself ... Such arrangements were subsequently very popular; everything was arranged, transcribed or varied. They constituted a source of continuing annoyance as well as of endless recrimination and lawsuits for composers and publisher.'[8] There is a grain of truth in this reception of arrangements. They were indeed largely popular spin-offs, produced in great quantities, as we shall see in Section 2.

But this popular dimension of arrangements can be seen in a positive light. It is time to take account of the people for whom arrangements were made: the performers in the home and outdoors, who ranged from amateurs to semi-professionals, and used arrangements to learn and to cultivate sociability and entertainment. For female amateurs, arrangements provided rare hands-on access to orchestral repertoire that they would not otherwise have played. And although composers and publishers railed against them at times, arrangements boosted publishers' sales, helped disseminate composers' works in fresh contexts, and generally promoted the emerging music industry while enriching musical culture. Objections to arrangements are rare before the nineteenth century, and when they do arise, they signal a change in the understanding of arrangements that we need to examine – a change in the underlying concept of musical works that gives rise to the notion of arrangements as essentially 'derivative' and (unless produced by the composer) inauthentic.

In fact, the principal composers of the era under consideration, including Haydn, Mozart, and Beethoven, participated directly in the practice of arrangement, for various reasons. Mozart produced his earliest piano concertos by arranging keyboard sonatas by well-known contemporaries (K. 37, 39, 40, 41, all in 1767; and the three piano concertos K. 107, in 1765 or 1771); and his Flute Concerto K. 314 (1778) is an arrangement of the oboe concerto he had written earlier for the Salzburg court oboist Giuseppe Ferlendis. As David Wyn Jones has argued, Haydn may well have arranged four of his 'Paris' Symphonies for string quartet himself.[9] In Haydn's correspondence with Artaria regarding the proofs of the *Seven Last Words*, for instance, we see that he was prepared to give the task of arranging to a musician he trusted.[10] In 1787 Artaria issued three versions of the *Seven Last Words*: the original orchestral version, a quartet arrangement prepared by the composer, and a keyboard arrangement sanctioned by him. Many arrangements from the era were anonymous, but from those that were signed we know that leading musicians of the time produced numerous

---

[8] Cited in David Wyn Jones, 'Haydn's Forgotten Quartets: Three of the "Paris" Symphonies Arranged for String Quartet', *Eighteenth Century Music* 8/2 (2011), pp. 287–305, 290.

[9] Ibid.   [10] See Hogwood, 'In Praise of Arrangements,' p. 84.

first-rate arrangements. They included Johann Peter Salomon (1745–1815), Johann Abraham Peter Schulz (1747–1800), Karl Zulehner (1770–1841), Johann Nepomuk Hummel (1778–1837), and Carl Czerny (1791–1857). Motivations to produce arrangements included learning the art of composition, getting one's name known more widely (this goes for both composer and arranger), financial gain, and pedagogical aims.

Placing Haydn's and Mozart's Arrangements in London and Vienna before 1800

London and Vienna offer a useful comparison regarding the purposes and roles of arrangements towards 1800. In late eighteenth-century England, concert life was emerging and the symphonies of Haydn were to be presented in public to great acclaim in the 1790s. Simon McVeigh, with his lens trained on the public sphere, finds that London was a focal point for the growth and early development of public concerts: from 1750 to the time of Haydn's departure from London in 1795, the principal foundations for the modern symphony-concert series were established, and Haydn's symphonies were at the centre. He notes that pricing and ticketing systems for these subscription concerts were designed to maintain social exclusivity, and that London's early concert life had to conform to the fashionable calendar of high society. The middle classes, once considered to have been prominent agents in this process of establishing the new order of 'democratic' concert life, seem not to have played such a prominent role.[11]

But into this narrative of emerging London concert life we have to insert the role of arrangements in the private sphere. Arrangements were a liberating force in European musical culture, especially in London and Vienna, because they put 'public' music into the hands of the middle-class amateurs, and kept the performance modes of this music flexible and plural.[12] As McVeigh shows, Haydn's music fitted with certain aspects of Londoners' taste – especially their taste for a mixture of learned and comic, for 'beautiful' slow movements, and

---

[11] For recent work on musical life in London around 1800, see, for example, Simon McVeigh, 'The Musician as a Concert Promoter in London: 1780–1850', in Hans Erich Bödeker, Michael Werner, and Patrice Veit (eds.), *Le concert et son public: mutations de la vie musicale en Europe de 1780 à 1914 (France, Allemagne, Angleterre)* (Paris: Maison des sciences de l'homme, 2002), pp. 71–92; and Sven Olive Müller, 'Kulturelle Gemeinschaften: Musikleben in Berlin, London und Wien im 19. Jahrhundert', in Franz Gratl, Andreas Holzman, and Verena Gstir (eds.), *Stereo-Typen: Gegen Eine Musikalische Mono-Kultur – Tiroler Landesmuseum Ferdinandeum* (Innsbruck: Wagner, 2018), pp. 140–5.

[12] On the contentious concept of the middle class around this time, see in particular William Weber, *Music and the Middle Class: The Social Structure of Concert Life in London, Paris and Vienna* (New York: Holms and Meier, 1976); and idem., 'The Muddle of the Middle Classes', *19th-Century Music* 3/2 (1979), pp. 175–85.

for the sublime.[13] These Londoners, who were not just an elite, could indulge their musical appetites in the home, with arrangements in diverse forms. As Gretchen Wheelock has noted, a good amount of Haydn's music was excerpted and played in arrangements, such that Haydn was well known to the English public before his first London visit of 1791.[14] One of the most popular forms of arrangement in England matched movements of Haydn's instrumental music to verse in settings for solo voice and piano or harpsichord. His 'Englished' instrumental music, which Antoine Berman would term 'ethnocentric translations',[15] served more purposes than cultural translation and preservation. It also created a context for the canonisation of Haydn, and the later reception of his symphonies as canonical 'works' – a function of domestic arrangements noted by James Parakilas.[16] The same canonising function pertains to arrangements of excerpts from works – for instance the numerous publications of 'The Beauties of [Mozart/Haydn/etc.]' that appeared in England during the late eighteenth and nineteenth centuries, which featured favourite operatic and other non-vocal repertoire by popular composers, fitted with new, sacred text in English, for domestic performance.[17]

Similar arguments can be made for taking a rounded view of Vienna's musical life and the role of arrangements in it around 1800. Jones explores the context in which Beethoven worked, including the symphonic repertoire of the period (c.1790–c.1830) and the features of musical life that shaped the changing fortunes of the symphony, from manuscript and printed dissemination to concert life.[18] The changing reception of Haydn's and Mozart's symphonies is charted, along with the works of less familiar composers, including Czerny, Antonín and Pavel Vranický, Anton Eberl, and Franz Krommer. His research reveals that the symphony as we know it – large-scale orchestral music for public performance – was in fact in decline. In the early nineteenth century, Viennese concert life was just getting started when it almost ground to a halt: it became difficult for a single composer to present work to the public on a regular

---

[13] Simon McVeigh, *Concert Life in London from Mozart to Haydn* (Cambridge: Cambridge University Press, 1993), chapters 7–9, especially pp. 131, 143, and 159.

[14] Gretchen Wheelock, 'Marriage à la mode: Haydn's Instrumental Works "Englished" for Voice and Piano', *The Journal of Musicology* 8 (1991), pp. 356–96.

[15] Peter Szendy, citing Berman, refers to making a past or foreign work conform to the taste of the day in a supposed national culture; see *Listen: A History of Our Ears*, trans. Charlotte Mandell; foreword by Luc Nancy (New York: Fordham, 2008), p. 46 (for the original French, see *Écoute: une histoire de nos oreilles* (Paris: Éditions de Minuit, 2001)).

[16] James Parakilas, 'The Power of Domestication in the Lives of Musical Canons', *Repercussions* 4/1 (1995), pp. 5–25.

[17] Discussed in Parakilas, 'The Power of Domestication', pp. 10–11.

[18] David Wyn Jones, *Symphony in Beethoven's Vienna* (Cambridge: Cambridge University Press, 2006).

basis because of high inflation, then invasion, and then the prohibition of large gatherings on suspicion of revolutionary activity. In the first decade of the nineteenth century, the violinist Ignaz Schuppanzigh led attempts to hold regular subscription concerts, but these were chamber music concerts. Writing in a Viennese newspaper of 1808, a correspondent noted the preferred small-scale and domestic context for music-making:

> In this capital, few houses will be found in which this or that family does not entertain itself with a quartet or with a piano sonata and, thanks be to Apollo, the once so despotically widespread card playing has fallen out of fashion … Yet so much is devoted to the so-called chamber music that there is little opportunity for full orchestral works, for symphonies, concertos etc.[19]

The opportunities were to worsen: in 1809–10, reflecting a general decline in cultural activity under the threat of invasion and subsequent occupation by the French, the number of symphonies performed in Vienna fell markedly.

Nicholas Mathew asks: 'if the genre of the symphony did not define Viennese musical life "around 1800" then what did?'[20] Part of the answer is theatrical music, especially opera (and often arrangements of operas for chamber groups). Another part of the answer is that the genre of the symphony was still very important in defining Viennese musical life – but in the form of arrangements of symphonies for quartets and piano and the like, rather than in full orchestral performance. As in the case of London, we need to put arrangements back into the historical narrative about the development of Viennese musical life around and just before 1800. The immediate stimulus for Beethoven's 'Pastoral' Symphony was Haydn's late oratorios, which people could get to know best through chamber arrangements, rather than isolated public performances. As Wiebke Thormählen notes, Gottfried van Swieten, who was president of the Court Commission for Education in Vienna and the librettist for *Die Schöpfung*, promoted art as part of a well-rounded education and personal development (*Bildung*).[21] His encouragement of active engagement with art sheds new light on the practice common around 1800 of arranging musical classics – particularly large-scale vocal works – for smaller instrumental forces. The act of playing domestic arrangements, one to a part, allowed not only musical development but the cultivation of social skills, through collaboration with fellow

---

[19] Ignaz von Mosel, 'Uebersicht des gegenwärtigen Zustandes der Tonkunst in Wien', *Vaterländische Blätter für den österreichischen Kaiserstaat* 1/6 (1808), pp. 39–40.

[20] Nicholas Mathew, 'The Tangled Woof', *Journal of the Royal Musical Association* 134/1 (2009), pp. 133–47, 147.

[21] Wiebke Thormählen, 'Playing with Art: Musical Arrangements as Educational Tools in Van Swieten's Vienna', *The Journal of Musicology* 27/ 3 (2010), pp. 342–76.

performers. The emphasis would indeed be on *fellow* performers in such arrangements, and in the prominent string quartet arrangements: men were the main performers on violin-family instruments around 1800. But one of the democratising aspects of arrangements at this time was the way they also allowed women to participate in an otherwise male-dominated musical sphere, namely orchestral performance.

The case of Mozart's operas was quite different. In German lands there was a veritable rage for Mozart opera arrangements from the late eighteenth century onwards (see Section 2), but not in London.[22] Although Mozart's concertos and chamber music were popular in late eighteenth-century London, and although he was a familiar name there, his operas did not 'take'. The Mozart opera arrangements of the early nineteenth century very clearly served a canon-forming function in London: they helped broker the aesthetics of complex music to the slightly resistant audiences. Thus, arrangements served the purposes of preservation and canonisation of music, as well as education, in late eighteenth-century Vienna, much as they did in London. There was cultural transfer between the two centres via arrangement as well. As we shall see in Section 2, Handel's name was similarly big in Vienna and London. But despite the rage for 'Giant HANDEL', as witnessed by the massive musical forces employed in concerts commemorating Handel in 1784,[23] around 1800, Handel's oratorios, like Haydn's symphonies, could be much more readily enjoyed when they were arranged for the home.

2 From Stage to Salon in Vienna circa 1800

Vienna around 1800 is seen as the cradle of the Classical symphony and other large-scale works, like Haydn's late oratorios and Mozart's operas, which are now canonised and celebrated. Since Eduard Hanslick's magisterial *Geschichte des Concertwesens in Wien* (*History of Concert Life in Vienna*, 1869), there has been much emphasis on public-sphere music-making in histories of Viennese music. But we have seen that at this time Vienna in fact reached a high point in private and semi-private music-making, in which domestic arrangements of large-scale music figured prominently. This is abundantly clear from the 1799 Viennese publishing catalogue of Traeg, explored here. This section focuses on Vienna in this era, asking what was arranged, by and for whom, and why. I also

---

[22] On Mozart's reception in London at this time, see in particular Rachel Elizabeth Cowgill, 'Mozart's Music in London, 1764–1829: Aspects of Reception and Canonicity' (PhD dissertation, King's College London, 2000); and Christina Fuhrmann, *Foreign Opera at the London Playhouses: From Mozart to Bellini* (Cambridge: Cambridge University Press, 2015).

[23] Claudia L. Johnson, '"Giant HANDEL" and the Musical Sublime', *Eighteenth-Century Studies* 19/4 (1986), pp. 515–33.

consider the social contexts in which arrangements for various chamber ensembles became extremely popular in the late eighteenth and early nineteenth centuries.

Who Were the Arrangers?

The principal composers of the late eighteenth and early nineteenth centuries often produced arrangements themselves. This was part of the process of learning the art of composition, in which they would also produce arrangements of other composers' works.[24] So, for example, Beethoven's pupil Ferdinand Ries's early musical training was mainly autodidactic, deriving largely from textbooks but also from creating piano arrangements of the string quartets of Haydn and Mozart, and of Haydn's oratorios. Ries later arranged works by Beethoven for publication with Beethoven's approval. Beethoven also entrusted the creation of arrangements of his *Wellington's Victory* and Seventh and Eighth symphonies to arrangers who worked for the firm of Sigmund Anton Steiner in Vienna.[25] Steiner's firm included publisher Tobias Haslinger; pianist, composer, and publisher Anton Diabelli; and composer and clarinettist Wenzel Sedlák. These men worked with, or as, publishers of arrangements on a largely ad hoc basis, before the time of in-house professional arrangers.

Table 1 shows arrangers of Haydn's London symphonies from the period 1794–1850, listed according to the city in which they published their arrangements of this music. There must have been many more arrangers of these works who were anonymous, or carried out unpublished arrangements. The prominence of London arrangers in this era is striking. London led the championing and canonising of Haydn's music through domestic arrangements. Most of the musicians listed in Table 1 were also successful composers, publishers, or performers. But they would add substantially to their income by producing very popular arrangements of works by canonic and non-canonic composers alike, and sometimes more than one kind of arrangement of a given work. Occasionally, too, they produced a series of related arrangements, such as the London symphony sets by Salomon and Clementi. The Age of Arrangements had its own cultures, practices, and key agents including arrangers and publishers.

Amateurs might carry out ad hoc arrangements. For an arrangement of an entire symphony or opera, one needed a good knowledge of music theory and

---

[24] Liszt, for example, transcribed the entire cycle of Beethoven's symphonies in the period 1837–65, a process he considered an important compositional task. See Domokos, '"Orchestration des Pianofortes"', p. 250.

[25] See my 'Marketing Orchestral Music in the Domestic Sphere in Early Nineteenth-Century Vienna: The Beethoven Arrangements Published by Sigmund Anton Steiner', *Musicologica Austriaca* (2021), http://musau.org/parts/neue-article-page/view/108.

Table 1 Arrangers of Haydn's London symphonies in the period
1794–1850

Arranger	Place of publication
Carl Czerny (1791–1857)	London
George Eugene Griffin (1781–1863)	London
Charles Hague (1769–1821)	London
Matthias Holst (c.1767–1854)	London
Thomas Powell (dates unknown)	London
Johann Peter Salomon (1745–1815)	London
Joseph Augustine Wade (1796–1845)	London
William Vincent Wallace (1812–65)	London
William Watts (1752–1851)	London
Domenico Corri (1746–1825)	Edinburgh, London
Julius André (1808–80)	Offenbach
Karl Friedrich Ebers (1770–1836)	Offenbach
Ludwig Venceslav Lachnith (1746–1820)	Offenbach
Ignace Pleyel (1757–1831)	Offenbach
Nicolas Bochsa (1789–1856)	Paris
Martin Pierre Dalvimare (1772–1839)	Paris
Louis Mesplet (1766–1831)	Paris
Johann Peter Spehr (1764–1835)	Paris, Braunschweig
Johann Abraham Peter Schulz (1747–1800)	Leipzig
Daniel Steibelt (1765–1823)	Leipzig
Friedrich Mockwitz (1785–1849)	Berlin
Carl David Stegmann (1751–1826)	Bonn
Josef Triebensee (1772–1846)	Prague
Christian Ludwig Dieter (1757–1822)	Zurich

orchestration; but it was a skill within reach of the kind of advanced amateur one encountered in Europe at this time, especially in Vienna. Composers might entrust the task of arrangement to respected musician friends who were not necessarily composers. So, for instance, in 1791 Haydn sent a keyboard arrangement of the slow movement from his Symphony No. 95 to his Viennese friend and musical amateur Maria Anna von Genzinger. When the score appeared to be lost in the post, he told her that she could make the arrangements of that symphony and No. 96 herself.[26] In the context of domestic music-making, who made a given arrangement was less important than that it was made, so it could be played. But this example also points to the agency of

---

[26] Howard C. Robbins Landon and Dénes Bartha, *Joseph Haydn: Gesammelte Briefe und Aufzeichungen* (Kassel: Bärenreiter, 1965), pp. 260–1, 265, and 267.

women in private-sphere music-making. In accounts of the late eighteenth and early nineteenth century, numerous female 'dilettantes' and amateur performers are listed, who would have been able to create, and may even have published, arrangements of complex music.[27] As Otto Biba notes with regard to Viennese musicians around 1800, the word 'dilettante' covered a broad range of skill levels from beginner to almost professional.[28]

The string quartet arrangements of Haydn's music that circulated in his own environment show the usual and acceptable ways of designating the arranger. The title pages of the quartet versions of *Die Schöpfung* (Vienna: Artaria, 1800) and *Die Jahreszeiten* (Vienna: Mollo, 1802) give the names of the arrangers, respectively Ignaz Mosel and Sigismund von Neukomm. The title pages of the two sets of quartet arrangements of his symphonies, Nos. 84, 85, and 86 (Vienna: Artaria, 1788), both give the credit to Haydn. Jones has persuasively argued that Haydn did in fact make these arrangements, despite scholarly opinion to the contrary.[29] Jones notes, further, that the extant manuscript parts of two opera arrangements for string quartet, *La vera costanza* and *Armida*, give Haydn as the composer of the music but do not indicate the name of the arranger. In those cases it is possible that the arranger was a music copyist employed by Haydn. The manuscript sources for both items are in the handwriting of two copyists associated with Haydn, his personal copyist Johann Elssler and a Viennese copyist Peter Rampl.[30] But arrangers were often anonymous and so invisible, which speaks to contemporary understanding of arrangements. Performance and enjoyment were the focus, not authorship.

So, many people made musical arrangements around 1800. They ranged from the composer to the music publisher; from the skilled musician to the amateur; and from the well-known and canonised icon to the unknown and unknowable 'anonymous'.

Destination Genres

Arrangements for string quartet were a typical part of the genre of the symphony in the eighteenth century, alongside the original works; and they were an

---

[27] See, for example, Johann Ferdinand von Schönfeld, *Jahrbuch der Tonkunst von Wien und Prag* (Vienna, 1796); facsimile ed. (Munich: Katzbichler, 1976); and Mosel, 'Uebersicht des gegenwärtigen Zustandes der Tonkunst in Wien', pp. 39–44 and 49–54.

[28] Otto Biba, 'Public and Semi-Public Concerts: Outlines of a Typical "Biedermeier" Phenomenon in Viennese Music History', in Robert Pichl (ed.), *The Other Vienna: The Culture of Biedermeier Austria* (Vienna: Lehner, 1999), p. 259; see also Gabriele Busch-Salmen, 'Geübter Spieler, Musicus, Virtuos, Instrumentist von Profession, Meister – Anmerkungen zur Bezeichungsvielfalt des Berufsmusikers in der Zweiten Hälfte des 18. Jahrhunderts', in Christian Kaden and Volker Kalisch (eds.), *Professionalismus in der Musik* (Essen: Die blaue Eule, 1999), pp. 98–104.

[29] Jones, 'Haydn's Forgotten Quartets'.   [30] Ibid., p. 289.

integral part of opera culture. A string quartet could easily be adapted as a string symphony, performer numbers permitting; conversely the four voices of a string quartet could realise much of the texture and harmonies of many eighteenth-century symphonies. So it is hardly surprising that Haydn and Artaria chose the string quartet as the destination genre (the one into which a given work is arranged) for the symphonies Nos. 84, 85, and 86 in 1788. Looking at Traeg's catalogue of 1799, one finds references to symphonies in the sections on arrangements for string quartets (including Haydn's later 'London' symphonies) and quintets (including six symphonies of Mozart and Haydn and three by Pleyel). In the section on symphonies, there are also references to quintet and quartet arrangements. For example, under Pleyel we find the cross-reference: 'NB. Pleyl Quint. Sinf. unter Quintetten und seine Quart. Sinf. unter den Quart. zu finden.'[31] At this time, string quintets were sometimes honorary quartets. But as we shall see, string quartets were not necessarily the most popular destination genre for arrangements: piano and piano ensembles were often preferred.

Regarding the choice of destination genre, of particular note in Traeg's catalogue are twenty-eight quartets by Handel ('Haendel'), which are mostly arrangements of overtures to his operas (the titles are given). This is symptomatic of the 'rage for Handel', which was gripping London in particular but was also transferred to the Continent, especially to Vienna.[32] This was also part of van Swieten's and others' interest in and revival of 'ancient' music at this time – another pronounced phenomenon in London around 1800.[33] But more generally these opera arrangements evidence a rage for things theatrical, and especially opera. Arrangements for quartets of music from operas and ballet are particularly numerous, with over forty-one entries, including numbers from *Il matrimonio segreto* by Cimarosa; *Der Apotheker* by Ditterdorf; *Una cosa rara* by Martín y Soler; *Die Entführung aus dem Serail*, *Don Giovanni*, *Die Zauberflöte*, and *Le nozze di Figaro* by Mozart; *Il barbiere di Siviglia* by Paisiello; and *La grotta di Trofonio* by Salieri. It was alongside this wider repertoire of arrangements for quartet and many other ensembles that Haydn's later symphonies, Mozart's operas, and many other works were performed and received.

Modern scholars and performers tend to restrict the definition of chamber music to original works composed originally for one-per-part performance in

---

[31] Alexander Weinmann (ed.), *Johann Traeg: die Musikalienverzeichnisse von 1799 und 1804* (Vienna: Universal, 1973), p. 21.

[32] On this subject, see David Wyn Jones, '"What Noble Simplicity, What Strength and, Certainly, Melody This Music Has": Handel's Reputation in Beethoven's Vienna', *Händel-Jahrbuch* 63 (2017), pp. 73–86.

[33] On Vienna, see Thormählen, 'Playing with Art'; on England, see Howard Irving, *Ancient and Modern: William Crotch and the Development of Classical Music* (Aldershot: Ashgate, 1999).

certain standard ensemble groupings such as duo, trio, string quartet, piano quartet, and so on. I have argued elsewhere that in Europe around 1800 a functional and locational definition of chamber music persisted, so that it was essentially defined by its performance in private and semi-private ('chamber') settings, rather than on the stage or in church.[34] The most popular type of arrangement, which converted a work for larger performing forces to a one-player-per-part version, suited for a smaller space, might be considered to be creating chamber music. The second most popular type, involving the rearrangement of existing chamber music for other chamber forces, similarly involves the creation of chamber music. Even the third type, where a string quartet gets expanded into an orchestral work, would still have been considered 'chamber music' in this era, after its most likely performance venue.

Traeg's 1799 catalogue helps define the idea of arrangement obtaining around 1800 as a means of 'creating more chamber music', since arrangements are numerous and intermingled with the rest of the chamber music in his catalogue. The catalogue gives us a better view of the total mass of arrangements produced in this era, because he lists manuscript sources alongside printed sources. So, for example, there is only one printed item out of the twenty-four items listed under 'Quintetti aus Opern und Ballets für verschiedene Instr. arrangirt' (quintets from operas and ballets arranged for various instruments); the rest are manuscripts; for the 'Quartetti aus Opern und Ballets für 2 Violini Viola e Vllo arrangiert' (quartets from operas and ballets arranged for string quartets), the same proportions pertain. In general there are more arranged works in manuscript than there are non-arranged works in Traeg. Missing from other publishers' catalogues of the day are the potentially vast numbers of manuscript arrangements, and, of course, those that were improvised at sight or from memory. The original chamber music, which one could purchase through Traeg and elsewhere, could readily form the basis of arrangements – the simplest of which involved substituting for the listed instruments others with similar ranges and similar technical capabilities. The wider possibilities for arrangement were limited only by the available instruments and by the performers, and their musical skill, lateral thinking, and imagination.

As Jones notes, Traeg's catalogue is somewhat idiosyncratic, with a bias towards the music of Mozart and Viennese local composers, reflecting his personal preferences and contacts.[35] Traeg was a key Viennese player in the posthumous canonisation of Mozart. He worked closely with the composer during his lifetime, and then with Mozart's wife, Constanze, after Mozart's

---

[34] See my *Cultivating String Quartets in Beethoven's Vienna* (Woodbridge: Boydell, 2017), especially pp. 7–11.

[35] Jones, *Symphony in Beethoven's Vienna*, p. 22.

death.[36] Mozart's music is the best represented among the arrangements in his catalogue: Traeg catered to the enthusiasm for chamber music in general and helped to make Mozart's music, in particular, more widely known. But this bias in favour of Mozart does not affect the way arrangements are represented. Traeg's catalogue gives a good insight into the relative popularity of different destination genres used for arrangement, and the most popular genres that were arranged (original genres) in Vienna around 1800. The catalogue is divided, following tradition, into the three main locations in which music-making takes place: chamber, theatre, and church. It is striking that the 'chamber' section is by far the largest and most varied. 'Cammer-Musik' is a massive section, which comprises a lot of what we would today consider 'public' music, including overtures, symphonies, concertant symphonies, concertini, and concertos.

It is also significant that opera takes over most of Traeg's 1799 catalogue – certainly the chamber and theatre sections – because there are so many arrangements of operas (the opera arrangements are listed in the 'Chamber Music' section and the operas in full in 'Theatre Music'). Italian opera is clearly the most popular genre in Traeg (as it was in Vienna and Europe more generally c.1800). A close second is German opera by local composers. In general locals are favoured in Traeg, and especially Mozart – so, too, Ignaz Umlauf, Peter Winter, and Vicente Martín y Soler. Of operas, Martín y Soler's *Una cosa rara*, and Mozart's *Figaro* and *Die Zauberflöte*, were major hits, as witnessed by numbers of arrangements. This probably has to do with their social politics (rags to riches) and sentimental plots, which appealed to a wide audience in terms of gender and class.

Reflecting the norm noted by Koch (see Section 1), by far the most common kind of musical arrangement in Traeg's catalogue is from large to small, where 'large' usually means opera; while 'small' most often means piano and voice – as in the arrangement of opera arias for voice and piano. But at the destination end, there are a host of other options in this era, including various types of ensemble chamber music. The largest group of arrangements that is listed by Traeg are the nonets in the Harmonie (wind ensemble) section. Under the larger chamber groupings are octets, septets, and sextets, including Haydn's *Seven Last Words*, priced steeply at 5fl. (about four times the price of other sextets in the catalogue); and there is a sizeable collection of sextets taken from operas by Gassmann, Grétry, Salieri, and Umlauf – in other words from popular, mostly Viennese opera composers of the day.

---

[36] On this topic, see also Dexter Edge, 'Mozart's Viennese Copyists', 6 vols. (PhD dissertation, University of Southern California, 2001), vol. 2, pp. 759–997.

String quintet arrangements were extremely popular, and show the crossover with the symphony that has been noted. Quintets comprising mixed winds and strings were also popular for arrangements. There is an entire category of mixed quintets drawn from operas and ballets. The same is true of string quartets. There is an even more sizeable separate section of quartets specifically drawn from operas and ballets; again they are mostly arrangements of works by local opera composers, and current operatic hits. These categories in Traeg's catalogue suggest by their relative proportions that there were fairly stable types of translations from operas and ballets to mixed quartets and quintets and string quartets. Just about all of these popular and prevalent arrangements would generally have been performed only by men, given their instrumentation.

In the trio categories there are numerous different types of trios but relatively few arrangements and apparently no stable categories comparable to the mixed quartets and quintets. From this we can conclude that the extra parts were considered important for downsizing arrangements, in order to preserve as much as possible of the original textures and complexity. However, a seeming inconsistency arises with duets, where there are again numerous arrangements. Duets for two flutes were a particularly popular medium for opera arrangements (again for male music-making). Duos for two violins were also popular. The two types are more or less interchangeable – the flute and violin sharing much the same range and technical capabilities. In this repertoire, the arrangements consist of duets and solos, rather than representing an entire orchestral texture, for which quintets and quartets are much more useful. Here, too, we find arrangements comprising collections of arias or 'hit numbers' as well as entire works. Mozart and Martín y Soler are represented, as usual. But Pleyel is one of the central composers in the entire chamber music section. A volume of arrangements by Johann Christian Stumpf is representative. Traeg's note for this entry reads: 'Favorit Gesänge aus der Opera Figaros Hochzeit von Mozart arr. für 2 Flöten erstes Heft ... NB: Auf diese Art werden alle neuen Opern der berühmtesten Komponisten für 2 Flöten arrangiert von Herrn Stumpf Heftweise erschienen' ('Favorite songs from the opera Figaro's Wedding by Mozart arr. for 2 flutes first booklet ... NB: in this way all new operas of the most famous composers arranged for 2 flutes by Mr. Stumpf will be published in a series of volumes'). These arrangements were primarily for entertainment (as in the re-living of popular hits) and sociability (as in the enjoyable sharing of musical ideas); but they could also serve for education (developing musical literacy) and obtaining a score-like overview.

Traeg's catalogue evidences several other categories that are not explicitly referred to as 'arrangements' but cater, broadly speaking, to the 'rage for arrangement' in this era. These are variations and dance music. So, for example, in the sonatas for flute and bass one finds variations including [Karl Jacob] Wagner's 'Variez über das Andante von Haydn mit dem Paukenschlag' (the 'Surprise' Symphony). Both these categories might well have involved both male and female recreation in the home.[37] But there is a still more significant category pitched at leisure in this period of revolution: Harmonie-Musik. These wind ensemble arrangements were intended less as domestic entertainment than as outdoor music, but they were also played as dinner music, as we see in the final act of Mozart's *Don Giovanni*. Here a Harmonie band is playing snatches of *Una cosa rara*, *Il Litigati*, and *Figaro* while the Don and Leporello await the stone statue of the Commendatore, invited to dinner. Under three-part Harmonie in the catalogue we do indeed see arrangements of *Una cosa rara* and *Die Zauberflöte*. Mozart was drawing on a well-established upper-class household convention, in a time when war made orchestras too expensive but wind musicians plentiful.[38] The most popular size of a Harmonie band was six winds, but an ensemble of eight was a close second. The most popular grouping comprised two clarinets, two horns, and two bassoons; but oboe and flute also figure. In terms of the repertoire chosen for arrangement for Harmonie, again it is the Viennese composers of Italian opera who figure most prominently; and operas, not symphonies, are generally most prevalent.

Keyboard music is such a large category that it requires its own section within 'Chamber Music' in Traeg's 1799 catalogue. This is hardly surprising for Vienna, which Mozart had dubbed 'Klavierland' in a letter to his father of 1781.[39] Under piano quartets we have Haydn symphonies in seven books; for piano trio we have twenty-three items relating to the arrangements of Pleyel's string quartets (much more popular than the symphonies of Mozart and Haydn at this time) and a symphony of Pleyel arranged 'par Beck' (Franz Ignaz Beck, a German violinist, conductor, and composer of instrumental music, contemporary with Haydn). Traeg clearly considers it important to name arrangers at this time, signalling that arrangement is being recognised more as an art than a craft, in which arrangements are not necessarily just a matter of convenience but sometimes also a matter of taste.

---

[37] Karl Jakob Wagner was a German oboist, conductor, and composer (1772–1822); he is a possible candidate for this arrangement. Traeg gives only the surname 'Wagner'.

[38] See also Christine Siegert, 'Semantische Aspekte instrumentaler Opernbearbeitungen', in Hans-Joachim Hinrichsen and Klaus Pietschmann (eds.), *Jenseits der Bühne: Bearbeitungs- und Rezeptionsformen der Oper im 19. und 20. Jahrhundert* (Kassel: Bärenreiter, 2011), pp. 10–24.

[39] Letter of 2 June, 1781, in Emily Anderson (ed. and trans.), *The Letters of Mozart and His Family* (3rd ed., London: Macmillan, 1985), p. 739; see also Wilhelm A. Bauer, Otto Erich Deutsch, and Joseph Heinz Eibl (eds.), *Mozart: Briefe und Aufzeichnungen, Gesamtausgabe*, 8 vols. (Kassel: Bärenreiter, 1962–2005), vol. 3, *1780–1786* (1962), pp. 124–5.

The section on sonatas for piano and violin includes a number of arrangements drawn from 'the best operas', the staples *Una cosa rara* and *Die Zauberflöte* coming up yet again. These Mozart operas appear under four-hand piano music, and one might be surprised to find so few arrangements in this category compared with the wealth on offer later.[40] Indeed, the keyboard section seems not to contain as many arrangements, relatively speaking, as the section listing the rest of the chamber music. However, the reason for this proves to be that there are so many keyboard arrangements that Traeg has categorised them elsewhere: they appear in the section on 'Theatre Music'. Here we find ballet and pantomime, Singspiele, oratorios, and cantatas arranged for piano; arias, duets, trios, and so on from German and French operas arranged for voice and piano; and even an entire journal in four volumes devoted to the latest opera arias arranged for piano.

Variations, this time for piano, are again borderline in terms of the definition of arrangement operating at the time. Variations can be a kind of arrangement, but one resulting in a composition so far removed from the original work that it was regarded as a completely separate composition. Nonetheless the apparent popularity of variations is another index of the rage for arrangement; and, once again, opera and ballet music were common sources for them.[41] The hugely popular category of marches and dances for piano includes a few arrangements. But in the dance music genre especially, many arrangements were probably made up on the spot by accomplished amateurs, rather than published. Conversely, in the categories of harp, chitarra, and harmonica music the published arrangements can be understood as a means of generating repertoire for enthusiastic amateurs who otherwise had little music to play.

Overwhelmingly, opera figures as the preferred genre to be arranged for chamber ensembles in this era. Traeg's catalogue also shows how opera and theatrical music infiltrates via arrangements into all areas of music-making – and particularly from stage to salon. His catalogue bears witness to a truly opera-centric culture, even though we think of this as the era of sonatas, string quartets, and symphonies, especially in Vienna. Opera buffa reigned, so it is hardly surprising to find many arrangements of works like *Figaro*. Arrangements fit well with the purposes of opera buffa – sociability, interaction, entertainment, and lightly-worn learning. But we do not lose sight of Haydn's symphonies in Traeg. They reappear in various guises (arranged for string quartet, piano trio, and solo piano) – an indication of the persistent emphasis

---

[40] Christensen, 'Four-Hand Piano Transcription', especially p. 257.

[41] On this subject, see Axel Beer, 'Die Oper Daheim: Variationen als Rezeptionsform', in Hans-Joachim Hinrichsen and Klaus Pietschmann (eds.), *Jenseits der Bühne: Bearbeitungs- und Rezeptionsformen der Oper im 19. und 20. Jahrhundert* (Kassel: Bärenreiter, 2011), pp. 37–47.

on *Bildung* (well-rounded education and personal development) in this theatre- and entertainment-oriented time and place.

Who Performed Arrangements, and Where?

Considering the culture of arrangements around 1800, we need to scrutinise the constitution of music's 'centres' and 'peripheries'. In music history, the home (chamber or salon) has been considered peripheral, while the concert stage or theatre was assumed to be the main centre of music-making in this era. But in fact the home or salon was much more of a centre than we have thought, and the culture of arrangements arranged for – allowed and enabled – a centralising of the home. Of course this did not completely destabilise or marginalise concert life. To a large extent the culture of arrangements reinforced and integrated concert life, which becomes especially clear when we consider the role of arrangements in canon formation.

A key factor in the intergrating function of arrangements was with gender. The string quartet and string chamber music in general was music associated with masculine leisure throughout the nineteenth century.[42] But the inclusion of *piano* quartet and *piano* trio alongside string quartet and string trio in Viennese publishing catalogues like those of Traeg and Steiner, and the tremendous popularity of piano arrangements altogether at this time, show an orientation towards women. Arrangements produced in Vienna around 1800 are oriented towards the piano, for various reasons. The distinctive powers of the fortepiano (including registral reach, chordal and textural capabilities, and timbral differ- entiation) allowed the broadest range of musical genres and styles to be trans- lated for domestic use.[43] But in early nineteenth-century Vienna, more domestic music for piano meant greater market reach: this was music in which women could participate, just as domestic music for strings was intended for masculine leisure. The gender bias in Viennese pianism at this time is clear from Johann Ferdinand von Schönfeld's long list of talented pianists in Vienna in 1796, among whom women outnumber men by thirty-six to twenty-five.[44] And in Ignaz von Mosel's list (1808), women outnumber men by twenty to thirteen. Most of these people are from the upper middle class or the nobility. Mosel's 1808 listings of Viennese performers on stringed instruments contain a mixture of lower-born and upper-class men. Women were scarce among performers of stringed instruments in Vienna in the early nineteenth century: Schönfeld lists three female violinists and Ignaz von Mosel lists only one, under 'Dilettanten'.

---

[42] Marie S. Lott, *The Social Worlds of Nineteenth-Century Chamber Music: Composers, Consumers, Communities* (Champaign: University of Illinois Press, 2015), pp. 13–18.

[43] Parakilas, 'The Power of Domestication in the Lives of Musical Canons', p. 17.

[44] Schönfeld, *Jahrbuch der Tonkunst von Wien und Prag*, pp. 3–68.

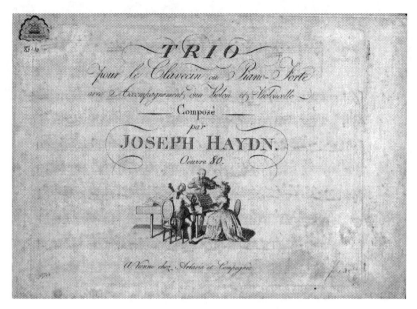

Figure 1 Title page of Haydn's Piano Trio in E-flat major, Hob. XV:90, reprint
edition (Vienna: Artaria, 1798). Courtesy of Österreichische
Nationalbibliothek, Vienna, shelf mark SH.Haydn.737

The amateur string-playing tradition was still going strong in early nineteenth-
century Vienna, but amateur keyboard playing was also flourishing, especially
among women. Mosel notes: 'An excellent [female] keyboard player is to be
found in almost every distinguished family.'[45]

Ensembles for piano and strings could include performers of mixed gender,
as depicted on the frontispiece of Haydn's Op. 80 piano trios (see Figure 1).
Female pianists in such ensembles often got a substantial and central role in the
private performance of this music. Hummel's and Salomon's preferred ensembles for arrangements of orchestral music were mixed quintets involving piano.
These arrangements allowed women to understand orchestral music in performers' terms, and to take leading roles including setting the tempo, giving other
timing cues, and delivering crucial melodic and harmonic material. An engraving from Vienna in 1793 by Johann Sollerer (Figure 2) shows a sextet of five
male musicians seated around a woman at a fortepiano. The arrangement
depicted has an unusual combination, including one flute and voice, which
suggests an arrangement of Papageno's aria from *Die Zauberflöte*, 'Der
Vogelfänger bin ich ja', in which Papageno blows on his pipes. In such
arrangements, the role of the pianist was often that of producing all or most of

---

[45] Mosel, Ignaz von, 'Uebersicht des gegenwärtigen Zustandes der Tonkunst in Wien', p. 52.

Figure 2 'Chamber music', colour etching by Clemens Kohl after Johann Sollerer, Vienna 1793; showing a sextet of five male musicians seated around a woman at a fortepiano, possibly playing an arrangement of Papageno's aria from *Die Zauberflöte*, 'Der Vogelfänger bin ich ja'. Courtesy of Gesellschaft der Musikfreunde in Wien, shelfmark Bi 1815

the orchestral texture. Participating actively from the keyboard in such works, women would gain a new sense of understanding and ownership of orchestral music, at a time when they would hardly have featured at all as performers in orchestral concerts.

A further integrating function of arrangements had to do with class. The 1825 diary of George Smart gives evidence of the kind of private music-making in Vienna at this time, and the contexts in which arrangements were performed. At one end of the house music-making spectrum was the elite 'quartet party', where arrangements were not so welcome. Smart attended such a party in the home of amateur cellist Ignaz Anton Aloys Dembsher on 8 September. The music played at such gatherings was typically complex, original chamber music, such as new quartets by Beethoven; and the audience and performers consisted of wealthy, musical, middle-class men (such as cellist Dembscher, and Smart himself, who sang). Of approximately twenty people present, only six or seven were women. The quartet players, meanwhile, were professionals or advanced amateurs: Mayseder (who was 'most perfect'), Dembsher himself, who played the cello, and two other amateurs. The works were 'most difficult' and 'admirably played'. Updating Mosel's account, but in the same vein, Smart reports that Vienna had 'an unusually high number of very competent amateur performers' and that 'largely through their efforts, private concerts came into prominence'.[46] Arrangements for strings alone might have been performed in such contexts, but were more typical in smaller, closed gatherings of men, such as the male family members who got together for quartet playing in Hanslick's account.[47]

But increasingly arrangements found a welcome home in the more diverse private and semi-private musical gatherings of the early nineteenth century. A case in point is the musical party that Smart attended on 17 September, at the house of Mr Kirchoffer, a 'friend of Ries'. Here the music 'was play'd by Amateurs, except the Leader, a young man, a Mr. Feigerl – in the conservatoire – taught the Violin by Böhm'.[48] This was a 'large party' and was very much a gathering from the middle ranks of society: Smart was immediately introduced to several women, and also the head gardener at the Schönbrunn Palace. The music, like the society, was diverse, including one of Mozart's 'Haydn' quartets, some solo instrumental music and songs, variations, and arrangements, including some of works by Handel. String quartet and quintet arrangements were also heard in these larger mixed gatherings, especially where an accompaniment was needed for an amateur production of a large vocal work but a small orchestra was not feasible.

The memoirs of Leopold von Sonnleithner (1797–1873), an amateur bass singer, mention such occasions in Vienna in the early decades of the nineteenth century.[49] A long-time family friend, Wilhelm Böcking, recalled Sonnleithner's own youthful engagement with quartet arrangements:

> But the young man already had such a mature judgement that he did not overestimate his own talent and preferred to become a capable jurist rather than a mediocre artist. In the autumn of 1813, together with several school friends, he organised Sunday quartet exercises in his father's house, which were diligently continued in the following years. The quartet arrangements of the overtures and symphonies, as well as entire operas and oratorios, which were very popular at that time, were soon also used and gave rise to multiple instrumentation of the voices, and to the addition of the double bass, a flute, and French horns (ad libitum).[50]

[46] Hugh Bertram Cox and C. L. E. Cox (eds.), *Leaves from the Journals of Sir George Smart* (London: Longmans, Green & Co., 1907), p. 107.

[47] Hanslick, *Geschichte des Concertwesens in Wien* (Vienna: Braumüller, 1869), p. 202.

[48] Smart, *Leaves from the Journals of Sir George Smart*, pp. 125–6.

[49] Leopold von Sonnleithner and Wilhelm Böcking, 'Leopold von Sonnleithners Erinnerungen an die Musiksalons des vormärzlichen Wiens', *Österreichische Musikzeitschrift* 16/2–4 (1961), pp. 49–62, 97–110, and 145–57.

[50] Ibid., p. 107.

At these musical gatherings of anything from four to forty people, women would have participated in performances of musical arrangements mainly as singers and pianists.

The memoir of Caroline Pichler (1769–1843), a Viennese historical novelist, offers a woman's perspective. Pichler was herself musical and owned a fine '*organisirtes Fortepiano*' – a hybrid instrument that could be used either as a piano or as a positive organ. Her memoirs are full of evenings of music-making, including some where opera arrangements are played. She makes distinctions between the treatment of an arranged piece 'as theatre' and not, and also between the performance of excerpted numbers and entire works. Thus, for example, in 1809, in the company of amateurs, she noted that a bravura aria was to be sung 'or to be produced in theatre at the fortepiano'.[51] She also speaks of more private occasions, in which theatricality or singing was probably superfluous, there being practically no audience. So, for example, she played piano reductions of Johann Gottlieb Naumann's operas, as well as oratorios, with the Viennese blind piano virtuosa Maria Theresia von Paradies (1759–1824), 'mostly without theatre and play'.[52] Possibly the degree of 'theatre' (acting, gesture, singing) depended on the presence and taste of an audience, while the extent to which excerpts were played rather than entire works would have depended on enthusiasm, connoisseurship, and performance skill.

* * *

Although arrangements helped stabilise and equalise musical culture around 1800, they brought with them several 'rearrangements' to the status quo that were significantly destabilising. Socially, the integration of women into the otherwise male-dominated sphere of orchestral music can be read as destabilising, especially where the female performer got the lion's share of the attention, with the part of greatest difficulty and even virtuosity. It was also aesthetically destabilising to have large-scale, weighty, powerful music miniaturised. There is a clear preference, seen in Traeg, for larger chamber arrangements of large-scale origin genres such as symphonies, operas, and ballets. Destination genres deploying the piano were preferred, not least because they could capture much of the original texture, if not the original weight and combined power of an orchestra. The exception here is the duet for two flutes or two violins.

In terms of musical culture more generally, arrangements were destabilising in the face of new ideas about music authorship and authority around 1800,

---

[51] Caroline Pichler, *Denkwürdigkeiten aus meinem Leben*, 4 vols. (Vienna: Pichler, 1844), vol. 2, p. 82.

[52] Ibid., vol. 1, p. 217.

witnessed in the growing number of jibes against arrangements.[53] In 1802, Beethoven described his era as 'a fruitful age of [musical] translations'; but a few sentences later he railed against those that were done poorly or against the original composer's wishes.[54] Musicians were starting to think of musical works as stable entities, compositionally.[55] The musical 'work-concept' was emerging: this is the idea – common in today's scholarship, analysis, and performance of Western Classical music – that composers produce original works (Urtexte) that are essentially complete at the time of composition. This conception of the musical work meant that the original version was starting to be considered necessarily prior to, more authoritative than, and thus superior to any arrangement; and arrangements were starting to be considered to be lesser derivatives.[56]

So much for Beethoven and certain of his colleagues and publishers. For European music lovers around 1800, arrangements *were* musical works – and they were better than the originals because they could be heard and performed over again, by the end user, in his or her preferred space. These music lovers were the agents against sole authorship, authority, and '(original) musical works' – forces that were increasingly making themselves felt. One modern theorist who contributes much to understanding how the culture of arrange-ment worked at this time is Michael de Certeau. His theory of 'everyday life' helps explain how people tend to make their own laws and rules in the face of institutions and norms, re-mapping and occupying restricted or carefully demarkated places.[57] Around 1800, 'arrangement' can be understood broadly as a cultural move that works to a certain extent against or away from emerging or established institutional norms. We see this in the Traeg's cata-logue, where arrangements more or less take over the catalogue, and upset Traeg's (and others') otherwise tidy organisation of music into its 'places'. Indeed, arrangement circa 1800 prevents music from staying 'in its place', or rather, its agents prevent it – the many types of arrangers just discussed, and the women and men who purchased or created arrangements and played them in their chosen venues in their chosen ways. Perhaps this is one reason why Koch noted in 1802 that theatre and chamber music were starting to merge. Stage became salon, in opera buffa in particular; and, in arrangement culture, salon became stage.

---

[53] On this subject, see Ladenburger, 'Aus der Not eine Tugend?', pp. 17–18.

[54] Ludwig van Beethoven, *Wiener-Zeitung* 87 (1802), p. 3916.

[55] On this subject, see in particular Lydia Goehr, *The Imaginary Museum of Musical Works: An Essay in the Philosophy of Music* (Oxford: Clarendon Press, 1992).

[56] Szendy, *Listen*, especially pp. 48–9.

[57] Michael de Certeau, *The Practice of Everyday Life*, trans. S. Rendall, 3rd ed. (Los Angeles: University of California Press, 2011).

3 Re-packaging the Classical Symphony

Haydn's last twelve symphonies are often considered touchstones in the development of 'public' music.[58] These works, composed for late eighteenth-century Londoners, are seen to represent a decisive break from the traditions of symphony composition and performance. Scholars have emphasised their 'public' nature: no longer designed primarily for private audiences at court, they were apparently geared to a much broader audience in public venues.[59] At this time, too, symphonies were becoming understood as touchtone 'autonomous' musical works, thought to reside essentially in the complete orchestral versions written down by their composers. Haydn's symphonies were among the first to be published in miniature scores, in Paris in 1801; and Carl Friedrich Pohl noted that the connoisseurs read these miniature scores at concerts.[60] Increasingly these works were thought to demand fidelity to the composer's intentions in publication and in performance – a view that persists today. A reviewer from 1829 went so far as to complain that arrangements of works like symphonies 'should often be termed *derangements*', the spread of which one should fear like 'the devastating effect of an epidemic plague'.[61]

These received understandings of Haydn's symphonies – as public music, residing primarily in complete, orchestral scores – require revision. In fact a Haydn symphony was often more easily heard in the home, as chamber music, than in public as concert music in the early nineteenth century. The reviewer cited, with his striking metaphor of the plague, was reacting to what he termed the 'rage to arrange'. As Beethoven had noted in 1802, this was the 'age of [musical] translations', an era in which arrangements, rather than the original versions of a given work, were an essential means by which that work was disseminated. This chapter provides a study of Haydn's symphonies transformed for the home in this era, in the context of where and how and by whom such works were published and 'packaged' to meet consumers' needs and tastes in the early nineteenth century.

Publishing Arrangements

For Haydn and other composers of his era, economics and public demand proved to be major motivators for producing arrangements. Haydn himself set

---

[58] This chapter draws on my 'Domesticating Late Haydn' (see n. 5).

[59] H. C. Robbins Landon, *Haydn in England, 1791–1795*, Haydn: Chronicle and Works, vol. 5 (London: Thames and Hudson, 1976) pp. 503–4; McVeigh, *Concert Life in London*, pp. 17–18, 69, 135–6, 153–6, 206, 214–21, and 226; and David Schroeder, *Haydn and the Enlightenment: The Late Symphonies and Their Audience* (Oxford: Clarendon Press, 1990).

[60] Carl Friedrich Pohl, *Joseph Haydn*, ed. Hugo Botstiber (Leipzig: Breitkopf & Härtel, 1927), p. 206.

[61] Ignaz Ritter von Seyfried, [Review of Beethoven's First and Third Symphonies arranged by J. N. Hummel], in: *Caecilia: eine Zeitschrift für die musikalische Welt* 10 (1829), p. 175.

up agreements covering publication of his works simultaneously in one or two countries; this was an attempt to overcome the lack of an international copyright law and to try to prevent pirates cashing in on his works, in the original or arranged versions.[62] Two publishers of Haydn's works in the era worked closely with Haydn, Artaria in Vienna and Broderip in London, on the publication of arrangements of his works. Others, with varying qualifications and degrees of separation from Haydn, cashed in on his works by publishing musical arrangements of them before 1886, when European music copyright laws became established.[63]

More than fifty publishers in around fourteen European centres published arrangements of Haydn's London symphonies in his lifetime (see Table 2 for the main publishers). The most important centres of publishing activity for early nineteenth-century arrangements of Viennese music were Vienna and London.[64] This is because they were major centres of music publishing in general at this time, but it is also a function of these cities' connection to Haydn himself, who visited London twice and lived close to Vienna for most of his life.

The division of publishers by city is not always neat: several published in multiple cities in this era. Schott, for example, operated primarily in Mainz but also in Paris; and Johann Nepomuk Hummel in London, Berlin, and Amsterdam. This was a clever way to get around local constraints on publishing, which pertained to Paris and particularly to London. London was one of the first European cities to develop music copyright; and in France there was an early development of performing rights. So cunning publishers and arrangers found ways around these local rules. This was also an era of self-publishing by musicians who may or may not have gone on to establish a firm, like Clementi (who did), Salomon (who did not), and Hummel (who merged his operation with Aristide Farrenc in Paris).

---

[62] On Haydn's own role in the dissemination of his works, see in particular Otto Biba, 'Joseph Haydn und die Verbreitung seiner Werke, in *Phänomen Haydn 1732–1809: Prachtliebend – bürgerlich – gottbefohlen – crossover* (Eisenstadt: Schloss Esterházy, 2009), pp. 154–61. On printing and publishing more generally in Haydn's time, see Günter Brosche, 'Das musikalische Verlagswesen zur Zeit Joseph Haydns', in Gerda Mraz, Gottfried Mraz, and Gerald Schlag (eds.), *Joseph Haydn in seiner Zeit* (Eisenstadt: Amt der Burgenländischen Landesregierung, 1982), pp. 270–5.

[63] The first international agreement involving copyright was the Berne Convention of 1886. Its core principle was the requirement that each of the contracting countries provide automatic protection for works in all other countries of the union and for unpublished works whose authors are citizens of or residents in those countries.

[64] Vienna was behind the game in European music publishing until late in the eighteenth century; see Jones, *Symphony in Beethoven's Vienna*, p. 27.

Table 2 Publishers of arrangements of Haydn's symphonies in his lifetime, by place

Place	Publisher
London (20 publishers)	Bates, Birchall, Broderip and Wilkinson, Chappell, Clementi, Collard & Collard, Corri, Dussek & Co. (also Edinburgh), Goulding, Hodsoll, Hummel (also Berlin and Amsterdam), Lavenu, Lee, Longman and Broderip, Monzani & Hill, Novello, Preston, Salomon, Walker, R. Cocks and Co., Williams
Paris (12)	Colombier, Duhan, Erard, Heugel, Leduc, Magasin du Conservatoire, Mus. Magazin, Pleyel, Richault, Schott (also Mainz), Sieber, Simrock (also Bonn)
Vienna (7)	Artaria (also Mainz), Cappi, Diabelli, Haslinger, Mollo, Steiner, Traeg
Leipzig (5)	Breitkopf & Härtel, Kühnel, Lehmann, Peters, Schmiedt & Rau
Dresden (2)	Hoffarth, Meinhold
Amsterdam (1)	Kuntze
Basel (1)	Gombart (also Augsburg)
Berlin (1)	Reifenstahl
Bonn (1)	Simrock (also Paris)
Breslau (1)	Leuckart
Mainz (1)	Schott (also Paris)
Offenbach (1)	André
Rotterdam (1)	Plattner
Zurich (1)	Nägeli

London led the way in developing the culture of musical arrangements – especially the re-purposing and re-packaging of 'public' repertoires for private consumption. London had the biggest market for Haydn symphonies in arrangements. Of course, there was a special association between Haydn, and particularly these symphonies, and London. But this large market share also had to do with the booming concert life (creating a demand for re-hearing a symphony at home) and theatre life in London; the flourishing music publishing trade; and, not least, the flourishing of domestic music-making. Some London arrangements, including those of Haydn's works, were even destined for public performance, such as high-profile examples from Hummel. Hummel made piano trio arrangements of Haydn's London symphonies in the period 1820–35; he also made arrangements of seven of Mozart's piano concertos for flute, violin, cello, and piano; and eight of Beethoven's symphonies for the same grouping.

In each of these versions, the piano part contains the main melodic materials and is designed to be performed alone (for example, by Hummel himself, in public) or in the chamber ensemble setting (with relatively easy parts added for amateur performance).

The thriving concert life in London around 1800 created a demand for domestic arrangements because concert ticket prices were high, and people wanted to re-experience music they had heard on the stage, or experience it affordably for the first time. We can see this clearly in title pages that read 'as performed in the Philharmonic Society concerts' and so on – a good example of packaging by a publisher who has understood the market and is riding on the rage for arrangements.[65] London publishers also paved the way in producing sets and series of arrangements, as did Steiner and Haslinger in Vienna. Beethoven was clearly interested in the London market, asking Ries to procure copies of arrangements of his own symphonies by Girolamo Masi and William Watts from London.[66] Paris was a large and well-established market. As in London, chamber-type works were starting to be heard in public concerts more often; again arrangements, such as those of Hummel, could be sold in a flexible form, which allowed for public or private performance.

In Vienna the situation was somewhat different. Concert life was not so well established, and publishers of arrangements were sometimes affording people the only opportunity to perform large-scale works – in the home. Here there was also a difference in that publishers were working with local names and products (Mozart, Haydn, Beethoven, and their works) and building their reputations (and coffers) on these names. Working with locals meant easier access to their work and potentially more exclusive rights. But this did not stop publishers abroad from cashing in – not at all. As far as arrangements were concerned piracy was standard practice.

German lands were altogether very important in music publishing history at this point, especially as regards Beethoven. Publishers of music like André in Offenbach were forging ahead with new printing technologies and techniques that would allow cheaper and better editions, and after 1800 Leipzig emerged as the greatest centre of music publishing in Europe. Bernhard Christoph Breitkopf was one of the first music publishers in Germany. He started out as a printer and general publisher, but from 1754 onwards began to specialise in music. Gottfried Christoph Härtel joined him in 1795, and the firm soon because a partnership, Breitkopf & Härtel. The firm moved ahead with the Complete Beethoven Works in the 1860s, and made its name around the Viennese 'classical' composers, publishing numerous arrangements.

---

[65] November, *Beethoven's Symphonies Arranged for the Chamber*, p. 108.   [66] Ibid., p. 105.

Table 3 Publishers of arrangements of Beethoven's music in his lifetime, by place

Place	Publisher
London (8 publishers)	Cappi & Co., Chappell & Clementi, Birchall, Hodsoll, Hummel, Lavenu, Monzani & Hill, Royal Harmonic Institution
Paris (7)	Imbault, Janet et Cotelle, Pacini, Pleyel, Probst and Richault, Schlesinger, Sieber
Vienna (5)	Artaria, Bureau des Arts et d'Industrie*, Haslinger, Mollo, Steiner
Leipzig (5)	Hofmeister, Breitkopf & Härtel, Bureau de Musique (later Peters), Kühnel, Probst
Mainz (2)	Schott*, Zulehner
Bonn (1)	Simrock
Braunschweig (1)	Musicalisches Magazin
Offenbach (1)	André
Saint Petersberg (1)	Richter
	*Bureau des Arts et d'Industrie operated in Budapest as well as Vienna; Schott operated in Antwerp and Paris as well as Mainz

It is instructive to compare Table 2 with that of publishers of arrangements of Beethoven's nine symphonies over the same period of time (see Table 3). More than thirty publishers in around ten European centres published arrangements of Beethoven's symphonies in his lifetime (compared with more than fifty publishers in around fourteen locations for Haydn). There is plenty of overlap in terms of the publishers, but it is clear that Haydn's symphonies were slightly more widely disseminated over a roughly similar period of time, and were arranged in significantly greater numbers. This doubtless has to do with consumers' demand for accessible chamber music. Haydn's London symphonies were immediately popular and entertaining; Beethoven's first two symphonies were likewise, but from the 'Eroica' onwards the numbers of early nineteenth-century arrangements of Beethoven's subsequent symphonies declined. This was directly related to the perceived difficulty of these works, and tells us that for publishers, entertainment tended to trump education as a criterion for arrangement. In an era of high inflation and high initial printing costs, publishers needed to meet market demands.

Table 2, like Table 1, represents the tip of the iceberg of Haydn arrangements and arrangers. Published arrangements were very popular, and were often reprinted, and also circulated in manuscript – either as copies of prints or as new arrangements, as seen in Traeg. So, for example, I have identified only one extant string quintet arrangement of Beethoven's 'Eroica' Symphony from Beethoven's time, and it existed only in manuscript, even though the string quintet genre was one of the most popular for arrangements, especially of large-scale works like symphonies (discussed later).[67] The fact is that around 1800 music publishing was a relatively new way to disseminate music in large quantities. Beforehand, circulation in manuscript was common, and it remained popular. Manuscript was a good option for any amateur who wanted to try his or her hand at arrangement.

Re-packaging Haydn's Symphonies

Arrangements sold well around 1800 because they extended musical works in ways that were meaningful for music's consumers, for example, re-purposing symphonic music as small-scale chamber music to invite social interaction. This casts doubt on the idea that the music of Haydn and his contemporaries resides essentially in 'complete', unitary works, in their original and definitive form as left by the composer – the so-called 'Fassung lezter Hand'. This notion fails to recognise the centrality of performance and pragmatism to the understanding and realisation of the musical work around 1800. We can see this pragmatism, and a recognition of the importance of arrangements to the reception of given works, in the tendency to re-issue certain works, such as the London symphonies, over and over again in diverse formats. Similarly pragmatic is the issuing of works with an indication on the title page that various alternative chamber groupings might perform the given arrangement, or indeed that a symphony could be adapted by performers as chamber music.

So, for example, the London publisher John Bland issued a series of Haydn symphonies from 1782 onwards in parts for full orchestra, but with the additional note 'This Sinfonie may be played as a Quintet'. He also noted that the symphony in question could be played 'as a Quartett'. This reduction meant that wind solos had to be omitted. Johann Peter Salomon departed from this practice with his arrangements, which go a long way towards accounting for the entire orchestral texture, but still took a pragmatic approach.[68] He first issued arrangements of the twelve London symphonies for piano trio in 1796–7, and then again in 1798, as quintets for string quartet plus flute with piano ad libitum.

[67] Ludwig van Beethoven [arranger anonymous], *5 simphonies arrangeés en quintett pour 2 violons, 2 violes et violoncelle con contrabasso* (Vienna? c.1810–20), University of Auckland Library, Music Glass Case, shelfmark 785.75M B41c.

[68] Detailed analysis is found in Hogwood, 'In Praise of Arrangements', pp. 87–101.

These 'quintetto' symphonies were then reissued by Nikolaus Simrock in Bonn, c.1801, with the addition of double bass and two horns, and a note on the title page that the double bass, horns, and flute are optional.

Canon formation was a by-product of arrangement, but undoubtedly important for Haydn reception. Arrangement, as a form of musical domestication, made certain composers household names and made the music accessible for amateur performers, including women who would otherwise never have had the chance to perform orchestral music. The act of familiarising oneself with the music by repeatedly performing it served to enhance and perpetuate understanding of the music, and familiarity with its composer, without regular concert attendance; for the budding composer, it also facilitated emulation.[69] Thus the culture of arrangement could contribute to the formation of the three main types of musical canon that William Weber identifies: the performing canon (the active repertoire of publicly performed music), the scholarly canon (of music that is taught, and written about in reviews and textbooks), and even the pedagogical canon (of music emulated by composers in the process of learning their art).[70] This culture not only raised the status of specific composers and works: arrangers and publishers could also connect their wares and reputations to increasingly famous names and popular works to boost their own income and status.

So it is that around 1807 the publisher John Preston in London decided to release an arrangement of Haydn's twelve London symphonies for flute and string quartet with 'an adaption or Thorough Bass for Piano Forte' by Charles Hague; this was to 'form a sequel to those arranged by Saloman [*sic.*]', as Preston put it on the title page. The arrangements of the London symphonies issued by the publishers Simrock (1798–1802), Clementi (1813–16), and Gambaro (c.1820) were all based on the Salomon concerts. The Clementi title pages announce the contents as 'Celebrated Symphonies Composed & Performed at Mr Salomon's' (see Figure 3). The Simrock and Gambaro sets add to the collection with other popular Haydn symphonies in arrangement for the same quintet combination as Salomon had used, both also including the popular Symphony No. 83 in G minor ('The Hen') from the Paris symphonies.

In Vienna, chamber music tended to replace rather than extend concert life, filling a void left by the decline in large-scale *Kapellen* in the late eighteenth and early nineteenth centuries. This decline was brought on by Napoleonic Wars, the invasion of Vienna (1809), and related very high inflation. Jones describes

---

[69] Parakilas, 'The Power of Domestication in the Lives of Musical Canons'.

[70] William Weber, 'The History of Musical Canon', in Nicholas Cook and Mark Everist (eds.), *Rethinking Music* (Oxford: Oxford University Press, 1999), pp. 336–55.

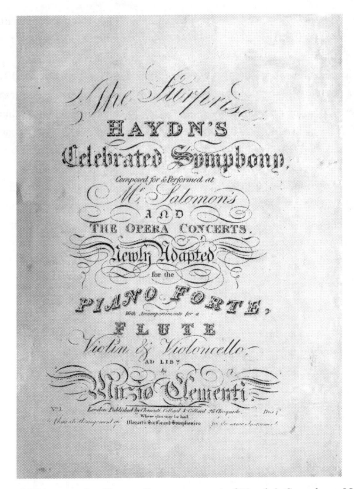

Figure 3 Title page for Clementi's arrangement of Haydn's Symphony No. 94 in G major ('Surprise') from his complete set of arrangements of Haydn's London symphonies (London: Clementi, Collard & Collard, 1813–16)

'the reluctance of publishers to issue symphonies' as a major feature of Vienna's musical life in the early nineteenth century.[71] But many and varied arrangements helped fill the gap. So, for example, Traeg's Catalogue of 1799 includes works by Haydn in the quartets section ('Quartetti'), which are described as '8 Quartett Sinfonien arrang.'. These arrangements were likely to have been drawn from Haydn's Paris and London symphonies.

The production of sets of arrangements of the twelve London symphonies was most common in the late eighteenth and early nineteenth centuries.

---

[71] Jones, *Symphony in Beethoven's Vienna*, p. 27.

Hogwood writes: 'In the case of Haydn's symphonies, while single movements of the earlier works were clearly eligible for transcription to a variety of media, the cyclic nature of the later works was respected with *publication in toto*'.[72] This does not quite represent the way these works were perceived around 1800. Of course, certain people were anxious to represent the works as complete entities, just as score publication was starting to reflect the understanding of symphonies as inviolable wholes. So Bland was concerned that the public should realise that his arrangement of a symphony 'Performed at the Nobility's Concerts' was 'Not a Mutilated Copy but the Intire [*sic.*] Symphony' (published c.1790, before the London symphonies, including symphonies Nos. 47, 85, 73, and 69). The violent metaphor suggests the increasingly contentious nature of arrangements and the emerging counter idea of musical works as original and unified wholes.

However, arrangements of individual movements of the London symphonies started to appear in the late eighteenth century, shortly after the works' first performances and publication. Of these symphony excerpt arrangements, second movements were popular, and especially that of Symphony No. 94 ('The Surprise'), whose startling second movement captured listeners' imaginations. The movement starts innocuously enough, with a pianissimo triadic theme. The fortissimo chord in bar 16, reinforced by the timpani, does not recur in any of the subsequent variations. So if you wanted a repeat of the joke – and listeners clearly did – then playing through an arrangement was a convenient way to make it happen. Even if a chamber version was not quite so astonishing as the orchestral version, the arrangement could provide a different kind of fun, allowing the performer to be practically involved in creating the surprise for unwitting listeners (see Example 1 for a six-hand piano arrangement from the late nineteenth century). This 'hands-on' aspect of arrangements of symphonies was certainly part of their appeal.

Choosing the Genre

One index of the popularity of the London symphonies is the twelve arrangements made by Salomon, and their spin-offs. Hogwood lists nine Haydn symphony 'quintetto' publications from the first quarter of the nineteenth century that could be classified as spin-offs from Salomon's initial 1798 publication.[73] Not all of them were complete sets; but it is a testimony to the striking success of these late works, and to the rage for chamber music, that publishers in Paris and Berlin as well as London got on the bandwagon.

---

[72] Hogwood, 'In Praise of Arrangements', p. 84.   [73] Ibid., pp. 103–4.

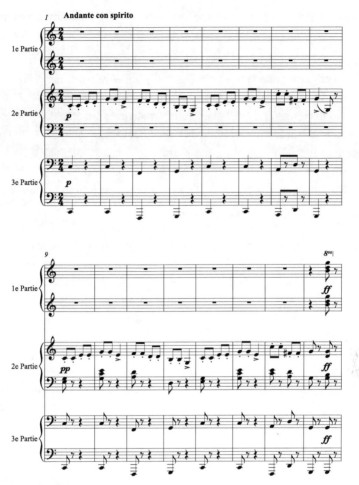

Example 1 Arrangement of Haydn's Symphony No. 94, second movement, bars 1–16, for piano six hands, by Renaud de Vilbac (Paris: Heugel, c.1874)

The quintet was a popular medium for arrangements at this time, especially of symphonic works. This might seem surprising, given that the string quartet was one of the most popular genres of chamber music around 1800. But the string quintet was often considered equivalent to the string quartet in the early nineteenth century, and it had the advantage of an extra voice (cello or viola), which was useful for translating varied and thick textures in arrangements of large-scale, complex works like the London symphonies. Wilhelm Conrad Petiscus, writing in the *Allgemeine musikalische Zeitung* (1810) on the virtues of string quartets, praised the viola quintet's greater resources:

> With good reason one selects for a good quartet the four well-known string instruments, which, on account of their uniformity of timbre, are most

capable of the most perfect unity. Quintets, in which the added second viola increases the power and variety of the composition, *belong to this genre*.[74]

After endorsing the sharing of melodic material between the parts that characterises 'true' string quartets, he observed: 'In this sense and spirit, Haydn and Mozart have written their better pieces – for example the quintets of the latter'.[75] Other writers of the time considered string quintets by Mozart and others under the heading 'Quartettmusik' in order to draw attention to and praise the genre, especially regarding the sharing of musical material between the parts. This sharing was considered essential to good chamber music, including a good arrangement, because it allowed every player to enjoy the musical interaction.[76]

In his 1799 publishing catalogue, under viola quintets, Traeg lists three sets (fifteen works in total) of arrangements of symphonies, labelled 'Quintetti Sinfonien', including works by Haydn (6), Mozart (6), and Pleyel (3). We can no longer determine precisely which symphonies were arranged, since these works were in Traeg's now lost manuscript collection, but it is significant that they came from the most popular composers of instrumental music of the day, including the increasingly canonised Haydn and Mozart. The keys of the Haydn works are clues to their identities: the six works are in D major (2), B-flat major, C major, C minor, and G major. They must therefore be the first six London symphonies, Nos. 93–8. Each of these quintets was priced relatively steeply, so that to buy all six would cost you more than twice the price of the more expensive sets of six string quartets in Traeg's catalogue. This suggests this item was valued highly at the time – more highly than chamber repertoire that is today more prestigious.

It is interesting that the keyboard transcriptions came first in Salomon's series. The trio version's title page reads: 'Adapted for the Piano Forte, with an Accompaniment for a Violin and Violoncello (ad lib.)', a combination described as 'piano trio'. But the entire musical content is contained in the keyboard part (as in the later Clementi and Hummel arrangements). Arrangements for, or involving, the piano opened up the possibility of mixed-gender ensembles. Although women did not generally play string and wind instruments in this era, they did participate in mixed chamber ensembles. Salomon and his followers were clearly aiming for the widest dissemination of these works. Later, in 1816–17, when Steiner released

---

[74] Wilhelm Conrad Petiscus, 'Ueber Quartettmusik', *Allgemeine musikalische Zeitung* 7/33 (1810), col. 517 (my emphasis).

[75] Ibid., p. 516.

[76] Markus Frei-Hauenschild, *Friedrich Ernst Fesca (1789–1826): Studien zu Biographie und Streichquartettschaffen* (Göttingen: Vandenhoeck and Ruprecht, 1998), p. 187.

arrangements of Beethoven's *Wellington's Victory* and then the Seventh and Eighth Symphonies, he, too, would prioritise piano chamber music versions.

Clementi's arrangement of Haydn's London symphonies was for an equally popular quartet combination of flute, violin, cello, and piano. During the period 1820–35, Hummel produced a large number of arrangements for chamber ensemble of symphonies, concertos, and opera overtures for the same mixed quartet ensemble that Clementi had used. He deployed this ensemble for arrangements of Mozart's last six symphonies and seven of his piano concertos, together with his selection of twenty-four overtures and seven symphonies by Beethoven, Beethoven's Septet Op. 20, a symphony by Romberg, and Haydn's Symphonies Nos. 44, 100, 102, and 103. Hummel also boosted the marketability of many of his arrangements by arranging most of them so that the flute, violin, and cello parts were ad libitum, and they could also be played and sold as solo piano arrangements.

Artaria versus Clementi and Haydn Arrangements

Comparing two different firms, one in London, one in Vienna, will illuminate the ways publishers created, supported, and sometimes undermined the rage for arrangements. There are certain overlaps between the firms of Artaria and Clementi, especially regarding their motivations for publishing arrangements.[77] But these case studies also point towards a split in the types of arrangements produced, which will widen as the nineteenth century progresses. On the one hand, in the arrangements of Haydn's symphonies that Artaria published, we have arrangements that are clearly destined for a private and domestic market, as were the bulk of arrangements produced around 1800. On the other hand, Clementi's arrangements indicate a trend towards a more 'public' and virtuoso type of piano arrangement, which will not dominate the market later, but will rise to prominence with Hummel, Czerny, Friedrich Kalkbrenner, and Liszt.

Carlo Artaria set the tone for music publishing in Vienna in the late eighteenth century, and built the firm's reputation around publishing the works of

---

[77] For background on both of these firms, see in particular Leon Plantinga, *Clementi in London* (New York: Routledge, 2018); Rudolf A. Rasch, 'Muzio Clementi: The Last Composer Publisher', in Roberto Illiano, Luca Sala, and Massimiliano Sala (eds.), *Muzio Clementi: Studies and Prospects* (Bologna: Ut Orpheus, 2002), pp. 355–66; and David Rowland, 'Clementi as Publisher', in Michael Kassler (ed.), *The Music Trade in Georgian England* (Farnham: Ashgate, 2011), pp. 159–92; and Rupert Ridgewell, 'Economic Aspects: The Artaria Case', in Rudolph Rasch (ed.), *Music Publishing in Europe 1600–1900* (Berlin: Berliner Wissenschafts-Verlag, 2005), pp. 89–113; and Rosemary Hilmar, *Der Musikverlag Artaria & Comp.: Geschichte und Probleme der Druckproduktion* (Tutzing: Hans Schneider, 1977).

Haydn and Mozart. The firm, which began life selling art engravings in 1770, started importing musical works from London, Amsterdam, and Paris in 1776. In 1778 Artaria switched to music printing, and one year later he proactively contacted Haydn and published a set of his piano sonatas (Hob.XVI:20, 35–9), inaugurating a series of over 300 editions of Haydn's compositions. Artaria also became Mozart's chief publisher and by this stage had established an international reputation. The publishing house was centrally located in the Kohlmarkt, with a branch in Mainz, and it traded regularly with other music publishing firms in London and Paris. As Jones notes, symphonies were not strongly represented in Artaria's stock, except those of Haydn.[78] Jones notes further that 'by the 1790s [Artaria] had established a commercial principle that was to be current in Vienna throughout the next century: economic success was linked with the provision of music for the salon'.[79]

But of course this commercial principle did not lead to the avoidance of large-scale works. For these, Artaria published arrangements. Like many other firms of the day, he cashed in on the thirst for things theatrical, arranged for the chamber. Artaria published substantial numbers of piano reductions from current operas and of individual arias (the pieces appeared between 1787 and 1804 with the special 'Raccolta' – collection – number). Also, in December 1787, Artaria, who was by then Haydn's principal publisher in Vienna, and indeed the most important of all his publishers, issued the composer's recent 'Paris' Symphonies in two sets of three: Nos. 82, 83, and 84 as Op. 51; and Nos. 85, 86, and 87 as Op. 52. Ten months later, in September 1788, three of the symphonies, Nos. 84, 85, and 86, appeared, arranged for quartet.

Jones notes that three intersecting characteristics of the commercial relationship between Haydn and the publisher are revealed in Artaria's publishing catalogues. Haydn's latest works were issued in their original form, and then as arrangements of chamber music that was already published in original form. Older works were also issued for the first time as well. To these, a fourth publication type can be added – the reprinting of earlier music. This suggests that for Artaria, and other Viennese publishers who did the same, there was little or no commercial distinction between the publications.[80] But in Traeg's catalogue, for instance, one finds that arrangements are sometimes priced more highly than an equivalent original publication. So the pricing and relative proportions of these publication types in catalogues of the time need to be considered when looking at marketing principles.

[78] Jones, *Symphony in Beethoven's Vienna*, p. 28.   [79] Ibid., p. 29.
[80] Jones, 'Haydn's Forgotten Quartets', p. 294.

Artaria included arrangements of various Haydn works – keyboard works, the symphonies, and the *Seven Last Words* – all in a drive to get more chamber music by a favoured composer of chamber music into the market. Of all chamber music by Haydn, the quartets were the best known and loved, so it is unsurprising that Artaria was eager to publish the symphonies arranged for string quartet. Shortly after Haydn's death in 1809, Artaria issued his own complete edition of the composer's quartets, fifty-eight in number, a local rival to the Pleyel edition. But even though Haydn had produced string quartet arrangements for Artaria, there are no arrangements included in this complete edition. Jones finds that this was a 'local act of canon formation', which 'reflected the increasingly lofty notion of the exclusivity of the genre in Vienna, one that was most appropriately promoted by omitting the arrangements'.[81] The exclusion may also have to do with the fact that the string quartet arrangements would have been less well-known to consumers; the original string quartets had been repeatedly republished by this stage, the canon formation already well underway.

Artaria was first and foremost a publisher, Clementi more a performer and musical entrepreneur. This difference in background helps to explain his different approach to Haydn symphony arrangements, and to arrangements in general. He was typical of the musical entrepreneur figure that appears in this time of emerging musical markets, taking part in many aspects of musical life as a composer, pianist, pedagogue, conductor, music publisher, editor, piano manufacturer, and not least arranger. This well-rounded career was a result of Clementi's natural talent, but also of a need to stay financially afloat in a fast-changing environment. In 1798, Clementi took over the firm Longman and Broderip at 26 Cheapside – this was a bit like Kohlmarkt, and at the time the most prestigious shopping street in London. Initially he held a partnership with James Longman, who left in 1801. Broderip had been one of Haydn's main publishers in England, and Clementi continued the relationship. Haydn had the right, if he came to London, to 'produce' any symphonies and quartets that he composed under the agreement with Broderip. But in the event, little of Haydn's music was published in London under the contract's five-year agreement. Longman, Clementi & Co. subsequently published Haydn's Op. 76. The first set of three, which appeared in London in the Spring of 1799, was made from an authentic manuscript of the work different from the one used for the Artaria & Co. edition in Vienna.

But there was another and much easier way to get Haydn's works onto the publisher's books: arrangements. Clementi's diverse background, including first-hand experience as a conductor and a composer, put him in an ideal

---

[81] Ibid., p. 297.

position to produce satisfying arrangements of some quite diverse music, most
of it large-scale, and much of it by Haydn (see Table 4). We can see that Haydn's
works in general, and particularly his later symphonies, are central among these
arrangements. Clementi, like Artaria, also developed a close association with
Mozart. He produced several arrangements of Mozart's large-scale music,
including six of the later symphonies, and the Requiem, in the late 1810s. By
this stage, Mozart's works were becoming more popular in London, and Haydn
was already a staple in the repertoire. In Vienna by this time, Artaria's domin-
ance was giving way to other firms, like Mechetti, Haslinger, and Steiner, who
all traded heavily in chamber arrangements of large-scale works, along with
much original chamber music.

However, Clementi the pianist was helping to shift the nature of arrangements, or at least to create a new kind of arrangement. Clementi was a virtuoso
pianist who engaged in a piano competition with Mozart in 1781. The piano
parts in his arrangements are destined for advanced amateurs, rather than
concert soloists, but they are designed to stand alone if so desired. The title
pages reveal the centrality of the piano in his arrangements, for example:

> Haydn's / Celebrated / SYMPHONIES. / composed for & Performed at M^R.
> SALOMON'S / AND / THE OPERA CONCERTS. / NEWLY ADAPTED /
> FOR THE / Piano Forte. / with Accompaniments for a / Flute. / Violin &
> Violoncello. AD LIB^M. / BY / Muzio Clementi.

And after the firm's address Clementi inserts his own advertisement: 'Where also
may be had / M. Clementi's Arrangement of Mozart's Six Grand Symphonies for
the same Instruments'. Ultimately, both firms produced similar end products:
Haydn's symphonies were re-packaged for smaller chamber ensembles and domestic use. But Clementi's works point towards the primacy of the piano as an
instrument for arrangement, and towards an era in which a piano arrangement can
become a stand-alone 'work' for concert performance, especially in the hands of
Liszt.

Piano chamber music was, after all, the most popular form for arrangements
throughout the nineteenth century. But whereas earlier in the century one finds
a greater variety of arrangement types, with piano chamber music occupying
a central position, after the 1830s the bulk of arrangements are for piano alone or
piano four-hands. Insight into the popularity of Haydn's symphonies, and
especially the late symphonies, in this form comes from Adolph Hofmeister's
1844 catalogue of printed music.[82] This third edition lists almost nine thousand

---

[82] Adolph Hofmeister, *Handbuch der musikalischen Literatur oder allgemeines systematisch-
geordnetes Verzeichnis der in Deutschland und in der angrenzenden Ländern gedruckten
Musikalien*, 3rd ed., 3 vols. (Leipzig: Hofmeister, 1844).

Table 4 List of published arrangements by Muzio Clementi

Haydn, Joseph, *Das Kaiserlied*, Hob. XXVIa:43, arranged for piano (Leipzig:
Peters, n.d.)

Haydn, Joseph, Piano Trio in G major, Hob. XV:25, arranged for piano
(Leipzig, Peters, n.d.)

Haydn, Joseph, *Die Schöpfung*, Hob. XXI:2 (Haydn, Joseph), arranged for
piano four-hands (London: Clementi, Bagner, Haydn, Collard, Davis, n.d.)

Haydn, Joseph, Symphony No. 82 in C major, Hob.I:82, arranged for violin and
piano (London: Longman & Broderip, c.1788)

Haydn, Joseph, Symphony No. 94 in G major, Hob.I:94, arranged for flute,
violin, cello, and piano (London: Clementi, Collard & Collard, c.1813–16)

Haydn, Joseph, Symphony No. 97 in C major, Hob.I:97, arranged for flute,
violin, cello, and piano (London: Clementi, Collard & Collard, c.1813–16)

Haydn, Joseph, Symphony No. 102 in B-flat major, Hob.I:102, arranged for flute,
violin, cello, and piano (London: Clementi, Collard & Collard, c.1813–16)

Haydn, Joseph, Symphony No. 103 in E-flat major, Hob.I:103, arranged for flute,
violin, cello, and piano (London: Clementi, Collard & Collard, c.1813–16)

Haydn, Joseph, Symphony No.104 in D major, Hob.I:104, arranged for flute,
violin, cello, and piano (London: Clementi, Collard & Collard, c.1813–16)

Krumpholz, Jean-Baptiste, Harp Concerto No. 6, Op. 9, arranged for
harpsichord or piano (London: Bland, c. 1796)

Pleyel, Ignaz, String Quartet in B-flat Major, arranged for piano, flute, and cello

Mozart, Wolfgang Amadeus, Fantasia in F minor, K.608, arranged for piano
(Vienna: Artaria, c.1805)

Mozart, Wolfgang Amadeus, Symphony No. 35 in D major ('Haffner'), arranged
for piano, flute, violin, and cello (London: Clementi & Comp., 1819)

Mozart, Wolfgang Amadeus, Symphony No. 36 in C major ('Linz') for flute,
violin, cello, and piano (London: Clementi & Comp., 1817)

Mozart, Wolfgang Amadeus, Symphony No. 38 in D major ('Prague'), arranged
for flute, violin, cello, and piano (London: Clementi & Comp., 1815)

Mozart, Wolfgang Amadeus, Symphony No. 39 in E-flat major, arranged for
flute, violin, cello, and piano (London: Clementi & Comp., 1819)

Mozart, Wolfgang Amadeus, Symphony No. 40 in G minor, arranged for flute,
violin, cello, and piano (London: Clementi & Comp., 1819)

Mozart, Wolfgang Amadeus, Symphony No. 41 in C major ('Jupiter'), arranged
for flute, violin, cello, and piano (London: Clementi & Comp., 1818)

Mozart, Wolfgang Amadeus, Requiem in D minor, K. 626 for piano (Vienna:
Artaria, c.1803)

Works of various composers (Corelli, Gluck, Haydn, Mozart, Sterkel, Vanhal,
Kozeluch), published as examples in Clementi's *An Introduction to The Art of
playing The Pianoforte*, Op. 42 (London: Clementi, Banger, Hyde, Collard &
Davis, 1801)

individual publications from 'Germany and neighbouring lands' for four-hand piano. Beethoven stands out, with three different arrangements of each symphony listed. But for Haydn's symphonies the numbers are even more impressive: forty-six arrangements for four hands are listed, by eight different arrangers. It is not easy to determine exactly which symphonies are represented in this list, which contains numerous re-issues; but of these, Symphony No. 94 in G major ('The Surprise') is clearly one of the most popular, along with Nos. 100 ('Military') and 103 ('Drumroll').

Arrangements of large-scale works for smaller forces and private use were tremendously popular in Haydn's time, as demonstrated in Koch's statement in part 1, and Traeg's catalogue in part 2. Indeed, chamber arrangements of large-scale works were so prevalent in the nineteenth century that to ignore them is to miss an essential part of the reception of the works in question. One of the main purposes of symphony arrangements, on the evidence of title pages and reviews, was to bring orchestral music into the home, for entertainment and education, in the form of chamber music. Composers and publishers alike recognised arrangements as a vital means of disseminating symphonies and theatrical works to a large and eager amateur market, when there was limited access to and limited opportunities for large-scale performance, especially early in the nineteenth century.[83] Symphony arrangements certainly served to extend concert life, particularly in centres like London and Paris.

It is difficult to estimate with any accuracy the number of arrangements of Haydn's symphonies over the nineteenth century, but surviving evidence suggests that the London symphonies were extremely popular choices for arrangement throughout the century. Thomas Christensen notes that Haydn's symphonies became one of the mainstays of four-hand piano music by the late nineteenth century: 'By 1871, one observer claimed to know of no fewer than sixty different published collections of his symphonies arranged for four hands.'[84]

4 Rearranging Mozart's Operas

> I looked on, however, with the greatest pleasure while all these people flew about in sheer delight to the music of my 'Figaro', arranged for contredanses and German dances. For here they talk about nothing but 'Figaro'. Nothing is played, sung or whistled but 'Figaro'. No opera is drawing like 'Figaro'. Nothing, nothing but 'Figaro'. Certainly a great honour for me![85] (Mozart to Baron Gottfried von Jacquin, from Prague, January 1787)

---

[83] For an example, see my *Beethoven's Symphonies Arranged for the Chamber*, p. 80.

[84] Christensen, 'Four-Hand Piano Transcription', p. 257.

[85] Emily Anderson (ed.), *The Letters of Mozart and His Family*, p. 903; Bauer and Deutsch (eds.), *Mozart: Briefe und Aufzeichnungen*, vol. 4, 1787–1857 (1963), p. 10.

Table 6 List of Mozart opera arrangements drawn from *Le nozze di Figaro*, published by Traeg & Son, in order of ascending plate number

K. 621 March from *La clemenza di Tito*, piano
K. 588 March from *Così fan tutte*, piano
K. 621 March from *La clemenza di Tito*, piano
K. 588 March from *Così fan tutte*, piano
K. 588 Overture to 'Cosi fan tutte', voice and guitar
K. 588 Aria from *Così fan tutte*, voice and guitar
K. 527 Overture to *Don Giovanni*, piano
K. 621 March from *La clemenza di Tito*, guitar
K. 429 Duet from *Le nozze Figaro*, guitar
K. 429 Duet from *Figaro*, guitar
K. 429 Aria from *Figaro*, guitar
K. 429 Overture to *Figaro*, four-hand piano
K. 384 Overture to *Die Entführung aus dem Serail*, four-hand piano
K. 298 Quartett, *Die Entführung*, flute, violin, viola, cello
K. 527 Duet from *Don Giovanni*, voice and piano
K. 527 Arias from *Don Giovanni*, voice and piano
K. 527 Arias from *Don Giovanni*, voice and piano
K. 527 Overture to *Don Giovanni*, piano
K. 620 Overture to *Die Zauberflöte*, piano

Hanslick recalled in 1860: 'Arrangements of overtures, symphonies, and the like [for string quartet] take the place of the four-hand arrangements that are now common.' He claimed that in 1808 the *Allgemeine musikalische Zeitung* was already advertising a string quartet arrangement of Beethoven's *Eroica* symphony, and soon thereafter of Weigl's Singspiel *Die Schweizer Familie*.[87] In fact these advertisements are not to be found in the *Allgemeine musikalische Zeitung*, but Weigl's Singspiel enjoyed great popularity. The appearance of the string quartet arrangement of selections from Weigl's *Die Schweizer Familie* (Chemische Druckerey, c.1810), first performed with great success on 14 March, 1809 in the Theater am Kärntnertor, represents a more typical choice for arrangement than the symphony. By 1810, favourite selections from Weigl's *Die Schweizer Familie* had also been arranged as Harmoniemusik, in piano reduction, and for keyboard and voice, and Weigl himself arranged selections from the work as a flute quartet.

[87] Hanslick, *Geschichte des Concertwesens in Wien*, p. 202.

In fact, the string quartet was one of the most common destination genres for opera arrangements, next to piano. This popularity continued into Hanslick's time, although the numbers of arrangements for piano had by then escalated greatly. Further evidence of this popularity, from Vienna, comes from the extensive music library of the Lobkowitz family, catalogued in 1893 by the family librarian. Joseph Franz von Maximilian, Seventh Prince of Lobkowitz, was a patron of the arts and particularly of Beethoven's music. The music library catalogue identifies 192 items as string quartets, compared, for example, with 147 listed as symphonies and 65 as quintets (for strings, and mixed strings and wind). In the list of string quartets, as in the publishing catalogues, there are large numbers of arrangements, especially of operas and theatrical works: for example, Haydn's *Armida* (1784) and *La vera costanza* (1779); and Beethoven's ballet *Die Geschöpfe der Prometheus* (1801), and incidental music for Goethe's play *Egmont* (1810).

Arrangements of operas by Rossini, Bellini, and Donizetti found here reflect the rage for Italian opera in early nineteenth-century Vienna. The contemporary arrangements for string quartet and quintet of theatrical music, especially recent operas, complemented the prevailing taste for theatrical pursuits of all kinds in the salons of the aristocrats and middle classes alike. Plots like those of *La vera costanza*, *Una cosa rara*, and *Figaro*, which tell or re-create 'rags to riches' stories, would perhaps have appealed more to the latter than the former.

Works or Excerpts?

What makes opera arrangements different from the symphony arrangements of the day? Overwhelmingly, opera was used as a basis for diverse kinds of arrangements, like variations on popular opera themes and potpourris of opera excerpts; while symphony arrangements are mostly of entire movements or works. But publishers took different approaches to the opera arrangements. In the early nineteenth century, the German firms of Johann André in Offenbach, Simrock in Bonn, and Schott in Mainz did not shy away from publishing arrangements of operas, including those of Mozart, for the smallest chamber ensembles. But the Leipzig publishers Breitkopf und Härtel tended to restrict themselves to the publication of large-scale piano reductions for two and four hands, of *Don Giovanni* for example. At the other end of the scale, the Viennese firm Diabelli, together with Schott and Simrock, rearranged *Don Giovanni* and other operas into pedagogical versions that are specifically reduced in scale and difficult to cater to beginners. Publications like Diabelli's 'Kleinigkeiten' (little pieces) and the series *Auswahl beliebter Melodien für das Piano-Forte mit Berücksightigung Kleiner Hände* (Selection of beloved melodies for the pianoforte with attention to little hands), together with the later *Recreation Musicales* (1840) and *Le premier debut* (1846), all take this downsizing pedagogical approach.

All these publishers tended to diversify forms of arrangement, with various re-workings of thematic material from *Don Giovanni, Figaro,* and other modish operas. Variations were produced continually throughout the nineteenth century, with new forms like 'Potpourris' and 'Quodlibets', and also 'Fantasias'. Table 7 shows the variety of arrangements of Mozart's *Figaro* published by Artaria in Vienna in the period 1798–1806. As in the Traeg catalogue, one sees that arrangements for piano do not dominate, but certainly appear alongside the ever-popular quartet arrangement and the duets for two flutes or violins that figure prominently in opera arrangements at this time. Particularly clear here is the way Artaria was cashing in on Mozart opera arrangements in 1806 – the fiftieth anniversary of Mozart's birth – using the title 'Quodlibets' (medley) to designate a collection of excerpts from favourite Mozart operas (*Figaro, Don Giovanni, La clemenza di Tito, Die Zauberflöte,* and so on). The works are realised in this format in four different arrangements: for string quartet (with the possibility of substituting flutes for violins), flute quartet, flute or violin duos, and pianoforte. This packaging emphasises entertainment and sociability – the enjoyment of hit tunes with whichever musical friends might be available – for fun rather than serious study. Overtures began to take on a life of their own in the reception history of operas. So it is no surprise that they are produced in chamber music arrangements. From 1815, more recent composers like Rossini and Weber tend to take over in the Artaria catalogue's opera arrangement offerings.

Publishers were aware that definitions of chamber music and the relative status of its genres were changing. This partly accounts for their application of the adjective 'grand' to certain arrangements. It represents a genuine effort to account for the scale and effect of these publications, which might be assumed from their sources to be slight or small. Sometimes they were in fact very lengthy and large-scale, like for instance the early nineteenth-century orchestral arrangement of Mozart's works by the Viennese composer and musician Ignaz von Seyfried (1776–1841): *Grande fantasie en fa mineur (f moll), tirée des oeuvres de W. A. Mozart et arrangée a grand orchestre par Ign. de Seyfried.*[88] But adding 'grand' to a title, which was common after 1820, was also a marketing ploy that suggested that particular chamber pieces were 'weighty' – long, and involving equality or complexity

---

[88] On Seyfried, this publication, and his arrangement of other works by Mozart, see David Wyn Jones, 'Mozart's Spirit from Seyfried's Hands', in Simon P. Keefe (ed.), *Mozart Studies 2* (Cambridge: Cambridge University Press, 2015), pp. 140–67.

Table 7 Mozart's *Figaro* arranged, published by Artaria & Comp., Vienna, 1798–1806

Date	Instruments	Title	Notes
1798	piano	Overture	
1801	voice and piano	*Figaro*	Entire opera; given to Francesco; Aria Collection
1805	2 violins, viola, and cello	*Figaro*	Entire opera in two parts
1805	piano, 2 flutes	Overture	Excerpts; in collection with other Mozart opera overtures
1806	2 violins (or 2 flutes), viola, and cello	Quodlibet [including *Figaro*]	Excerpts; in collection with other Mozart operas
1806	flute, violin, viola, and cello	Quodlibet [including *Figaro*]	Excerpts; in collection with other Mozart operas
1806	2 flutes or 2 violins	Quodlibet [including *Figaro*]	Excerpts; in collection with other Mozart operas
1806	piano	Quodlibet [including *Figaro*]	Excerpts; in collection with other Mozart operas
1806	2 flutes or 2 violins	*Figaro*	Released at the same time as other versions for the same instrumentation of other Mozart operas
1806	2 flutes or 2 violins	*Figaro*	Excerpts and in a collection from all of Mozart's operas

of part writing – even when the arrangements in question in fact exhibited no such markers of grandeur.[89]

Concurrently, there was a shift from arrangements of selected hits towards the publication of arrangements of entire operas.[90] By 1815, for example, Mozart's *Die Entführung aus dem Serail*, *Die Zauberflöte*, *Don Giovanni*, *Le nozze di Figaro*, *Così fan tutte*, *Idomeneo*, and *La clemenza di Tito* were all available to Viennese music lovers in string quartet and quintet arrangements. These were catalogued by Artaria, for example, as 'Arien, Overturen und ganze Operen in Quartetten'. This phenomenon of publishing entire operas in arrangement signals a new awareness of how opera arrangements related to 'works' – and a sense of arrangements as bona fide works in themselves.

Following the trend of more monumental and weighty packaging of opera arrangements, sets of arrangements of operas now started to appear. This is an aspect of canon formation, like the sets of Haydn and Beethoven symphonies in arrangements discussed in Section 3, in which publishers start to present Mozart's operas, in particular, as an aspect of a larger oeuvre. What happens to the arranger in this 'packaging' process? The answer again varies, depending on the arranger and publisher. So, for example, Schott, André, Simrock, and Breitkopf tended to put the names of arrangers on the title page from the outset. On the other hand, Artaria seldom mentioned the arranger. Before Diabelli founded his own publishing house he had already published over 110 compositions or arrangements with Chemischen Druckery and Steiner. He tended to do his own arranging, rather than bring in others, and he advertised this on the title pages. This was part of a larger trend: increasingly, well-known composers and performers, like Hummel, Czerny, and Liszt, turned their hands to arranging, for various reasons; and when they did so, they naturally wanted their names acknowledged on title pages.

Opera *ohne Worte*: Use and Functions of Arrangements

In 1811 Artaria released *Die Entführung*, *Così*, and *Tito* in editions for solo piano '*mit Text*'; and in 1814 *Fidelio* '*mit Text*'.[91] This was typical of such editions, and was not announced on the respective title pages. Unlike the piano

---

[89] See the anonymous review of the 'Grand Trios' Op. 43 of Adalbert Gyrowetz in *Allgemeine musikalische Zeitung* 8/47 (1806), col. 751; for an early nineteenth-century Mozart example, see Ignaz von Seyfried, *Grande fantasie en fa mineur (f moll), tirée des oeuvres de W. A. Mozart et arrangée à grand orchestre par Ign. de Seyfried*, ... no. 2. (Leipzig: Breitkopf & Härtel, n.d.); Austrian National Library Musiksammlung, shelfmark L18.Kaldeck MS41753-4°.

[90] Wiebke Thomählen, 'Art, Education and Entertainment', pp. 344–5.

[91] For a full scan of Artaria's 1814 solo piano arrangement of *Fidelio* with text, see: www .beethoven.de/en/media/view/4529268960788480/scan/0.

Example 2 Beethoven's incidental music to Goethe's *Egmont*, arranged in full for string quartet by Alexander Brand for Simrock (1826). No. 8, Melodrama, bars 1–14. Courtesy of Beethoven-Haus, Bonn

reductions, however, the instrumental arrangements of operas 1750–1850 are largely without text. Beethoven's incidental music to *Egmont*, arranged in full for string quartet by Alexander Brand for Simrock in 1826, with text, was highly unusual. Example 2 is a score version of Egmont's melodrama drawn from the original string quartet parts, which contain the original text in all parts so that all players can follow the vocal cues. The reason for this exceptional provision of text is quite clear: the melodrama of this time was a technique of combining spoken recitation with short pieces of accompanying music. The two components are mutually reinforcing in conveying the substance of the original drama, in this case Egmont's drifting off to sleep on the eve of his death.[92] To publish music without text simply would not make sense dramatically.

But there are many *ohne Worte* (with words omitted) arrangements for string quartet (and other ensembles) of operas and other texted theatrical works in this era. It might be tempting to consider the *ohne Worte* arrangements of opera as a phenomenon of the Romantic movement, in which thinkers like E. T. A. Hoffmann espoused the Romantic nature of purely instrumental music, for its ability to convey drama and because 'its sole subject is the infinite'.[93] But in fact most of these versions were produced for two very pragmatic principal reasons: to provide yet more chamber music (especially string quartets) for Mozart fans and string quartet amateurs; and to provide a small-scale accompaniment for domestic singing parties, where a mini-opera might be produced. Thus we read in an advertisement from 1800 for *Figaro* arranged for string quartet:

> This opera is here completely transcribed into quartets, which combine the double advantage that they 1. satisfy the admirers of Mozart's music as quartets by themselves; but also 2. can be used as accompaniment to the vocal parts instead of the instrumental parts, either alone, or with the piano reduction. Transferred in this way, the following have already been published by this publisher: DON JUAN, TITUS, DIE ENTFÜHRUNG and so forth.[94]

An example of the second use of arrangements is mentioned in Sonnleithner's recollections of Viennese musical life in the early nineteenth century, published from 1861 to 1863. Sonnleithner was a prominent personality on the Viennese musical scene, who studied music and played several instruments. In the period 1815–24, he was the leader of a celebrated concert series held by his father at the family home. His recollections cover some twenty-five salons, including the early nineteenth-century musical gatherings of Field Marshall Lieutenant Schall von Falkenhorst, which demonstrate the centrality of string quartets to private and semi-private music-making at the time.[95] In such salons of the early nineteenth century, vocal music was often accompanied by a quartet or quintet arrangement. In the case of Falkenhorst, Sonnleithner cited the examples of the finales of *Don Giovanni* and *Così fan tutte*, each of which was accompanied by a quintet. The repertoire and performing forces in these salons tended to expand, as did the audience and venues. The large number of good string players in

[92] See also Daniela Kaleva, 'Beethoven and Melodrama', *Musicology Australia* 23/1 (2000), pp. 49–75.

[93] E. T. A. Hoffmann, 'Recension', *Allgemeine musikalische Zeitung* 12/40 (1810), col. 631.

[94] Mozart, *Le noce di Figaro (Die Hochzeit des Figaro), Opera de W. A. Mozart arrangée en quatuors à deux violons, alto & violoncelle, livre I et II* (Bonn: Simrock, 1800).

[95] Böcking, 'Leopold von Sonnleithners Erinnerungen', p. 157.

Vienna and the thirst for quartet and quintet music meant that such chamber music flourished. But contemporary arrangements for string quartet and quintet of theatrical music, especially recent operas, also satisfied the prevailing taste for theatrical pursuits of all kinds in the salon.[96] In the main such arrangements were dominated by male performers, who played in string quartets and quintets, with or without the addition of winds. But women could take part as singers.

Despite their pragmatic intentions, these arrangements of vocal music for instrumental chamber ensembles also foreshadow the Romantic perception of instrumental music as primary – because it could take the listener beyond verbal meanings. *Don Giovanni* for string quartet, for example, arguably affords the listener a more compelling experience of the sublime for the lack of specific referents. The listener's fantasy is set in play. A review of an 1828 reprint of an anonymous 1807 piano quartet arrangement of Beethoven's *Eroica* symphony suggests how such arrangements could inspire apprehension of the sublime in the absence of an orchestra. This reviewer piles up visual metaphors suggesting that the onus lay on the listener to 'perform' the work, via imaginative reconstruction:

> The copy of a giant tableau; a colossal statue on a reduced scale; Caesar's portrait shrunk by the pantograph; an antique bust of Carrara marble made over as a plaster cast. – One is readily satisfied, however, with a half-accurate silhouette when one cannot have the original. Then fantasy begins its sweet play, and all the world certainly knows the beneficial effect of the powers of imagination and recollection.[97]

The 'wordless' piano arrangements of the time were explicitly intended as such. They can be understood with reference to the reviewer's idea that the listener essentially 'completes' the work in his or her imagination. These arrangements gained in popularity in the first half of the nineteenth century, to the point where publishers began to omit the title-page message that these piano arrangements did not have text, perhaps seeing it as no longer necessary.

In the first decade of the nineteenth century the Viennese publisher Chemischen Druckerey's release of the *Journal für Quartetten Liebhaber* (*Journal for Quartet Amateurs*) was a sign of the times. The twenty-four volumes of this journal, issued in the years 1807–10, were directed at the substantial market of performers who needed something less challenging than the quartets of Beethoven, or the more difficult works of Haydn, Mozart, or the more demanding French composers'

---

[96] See also Dorothea Link, 'Vienna's Theatrical and Musical Life, 1783–92, as Reported by Count Karl Zinzendorf', *Journal of the Royal Musical Association* 122/2 (1997), pp. 205–57.

[97] *Allgemeiner musikalischer Anzeiger* 1 (1829), p. 199; Wayne M. Senner, Robin Wallace, and William Meredith (eds.), *The Critical Reception of Beethoven's Compositions by His German Contemporaries*, 2 vols. (Lincoln: University of Nebraska, 1999 and 2001), vol. 2, p. 41.

Example 3 *Journal für Quartetten Liebhaber*, trio from Beethoven's *Fidelio*, Act I No. 3, first version arranged for string quartet, bars 1–14. Courtesy of Beethoven-Haus, Bonn

work. The music in this series of journals consists exclusively of arrangements from contemporary operas, ballets, and pantomimes – hit tunes of the day. The composers represented are the popular composers of the day, including Mozart, Luigi Cherubini, and Christoph Willibald Gluck. Beethoven is featured in the sixth volume, with a trio from *Fidelio*, Act I No. 3, first version (Example 3). It is notable that the first version features here; this trio was replaced by a quartet in the 1814 version. The earlier version of the opera has enjoyed an 'afterlife' in such arrangements, although it is today largely considered to have been a flop.

Some string quartet arrangements were dominated by the first violin, but as we see in Example 3, arrangers usually took care to provide opportunities for interaction and exchange; thus, at least ideally, these arrangements also fostered sociability. Another example of a string quartet arrangement in which all parts have interaction and interest is 'Porgi amor' from *Figaro* (Cavatina, No. 11), arranged for string quartet in Artaria's complete arrangement of *Figaro*.[98] The aria is the first for Countess Almaviva, and so the arrangement unsurprisingly spotlights the first violin part, carrying the main melodic material in place of the

---

[98] Wolfgang Amadeus Mozart, *Die Hochzeit des Figaro: Le nozze di Figaro in quartetti per due violini, viole e violoncello dal Sigr. W. A. Mozart.* (Vienna: Artaria e Compagni, n.d.); Österreichischen Nationalbibliothek Musiksammlung, shelf mark MS14662-4°.

Example 4 'Porgi amour' from Figaro (Cavatina, No. 11), arranged for string quartet in Artaria's complete arrangement of *Figaro*, bars 1–25. Courtesy of Musiksammlung der Österreichischen Nationalbibliothek

solo voice. But Mozart's arias are, as James Webster describes them, multivalent, and the rich orchestral texture proves rewarding for all the players (Example 4).[99] Mozart was fond of representing the different perspectives of

---

[99] James Webster, 'The Analysis of Mozart's Arias', in Cliff Eisen (ed.), *Mozart Studies 2* (Oxford: Clarendon Press, 1991), pp. 101–99.

characters in ensemble numbers, which translate readily into the instrumental chamber music parts. Taste and moral sentiment – no longer directly accessible through words in these purely instrumental arrangements – could also be promoted through the performance of one-to-a-part arrangements of morally instructive vocal music, such as Haydn's *Die Schöpfung* and Mozart's *Figaro*.[100]

However, performers were interacting not only with theatrical plots of the morally uplifting kind. The performance of favourite operas in quartet and quintet arrangements would also have provided an opportunity to engage with some favourite 'forbidden' roles: the rakish Count Almaviva in *Figaro*, for instance, or Don Giovanni. Role-play in instrumental arrangements was perceived as a more innocuous pursuit than acting in plays or reading and discussing potentially inflammatory literature, but the door was open for covert enjoyment of dubious characters and villains. Nor did performers of these arrangements necessarily perceive themselves to be engaging with exemplars of musical beauty. Haydn's *Die Schöpfung,* Mozart's *Don Giovanni*, and Beethoven's 'Eroica' Symphony would also have been considered by contemporaries to offer fine examples of the musical sublime, owing to their canonical texts, complex textures, and the awe and sense of incommensurability they invoke. The sublime was a powerful, shocking, manipulative category of aesthetic experience, with the potential to overcome the beholder or listener, and was understood largely in opposition to the beautiful.[101] Example 5, drawn from Mollo's string quartet arrangement of *Don Giovanni*, exhibits several aspects of the musical sublime, even in this small-scale format, such as stark contrasts of dynamics and register, thought to give rise to a sense of incommensurability, associated with the 'mathematical sublime'.[102] Oddly enough, the voice of the Commendatore is not a bass but a treble: first violin. But the angular lines of this voice are nonetheless rendered, and the setting is all the more *Unheimlich* (uncanny) and menacing for the blending of voices: in this scene Don Giovanni increasingly takes on the angular vocality of the Commendatore, after his fate is sealed in the crucial

---

[100] Thormählen, 'Art, Education and Entertainment', pp. 345–6, 348–60; Mozart, *"Il Don Giovanni": Grand opera ridotta in quartetti per due violini, viola e basso del Sigr W. A. Mozart* (Vienna: Mollo, n.d.); Österreichischen Nationalbibliothek Musiksammlung, shelf mark MS31926-4°.

[101] For a relevant summary, see Keith Chapin, s.v. 'Sublime', in Caryl Clark and Sarah Day-O'Connell (eds.), *The Cambridge Haydn Encyclopedia* (Cambridge: Cambridge University Press, 2019), pp. 352–5.

[102] On the mathematical sublime, see James Webster, 'The Creation, Haydn's Late Vocal Music, and the Musical Sublime', in Elaine Sisman (ed.), *Haydn and His World* (Princeton: Princeton University Press, 1997), pp. 57–102, 59–60.

Example 5 Excerpt from the Finale in Mollo's string quartet arrangement of *Don Giovanni*, Act 2, Scene 15, bars 1–21. Courtesy of Musiksammlung der Österreichischen Nationalbibliothek

moment when he gives the Commendatore his hand – a scene often depicted on title pages of published arrangements at this time (see Figure 4).

Figure 4 Hopwood's engraving from *Don Giovanni* (Act 2, Scene 14) for
Goulding D'Almaine, Potter and Co.'s series of engraved editions of
arrangements of selections from Mozart's operas, London, 1816. Image
© Karin Breitner, ed., *Katalog der Sammlung Anthony van Hoboken in der
Musiksammlung der Österreichischen Nationalbibliothek*

Title Pages, Paratexts, and Canon Formation

The title pages of the chamber music editions of Mozart's operas published in
the late eighteenth and early nineteenth centuries (including arrangements of
them) furnish much evidence about the process of Mozart canon formation and
the construction of his works as 'monumental'.[103] We can understand title pages
as part of the 'paratext' of the opera arrangements – the 'liminal devices and
conventions' that surround the main (musical) text. Elements of the title page
help to set the tone of the transaction between the composer and publisher, and
the reader or performer.[104] Clever use by publishers of title page elements to

---

[103] This section draws on my 'Marketing Ploys, Monuments, and Myths: Reading Early Title Pages
of Mozart's Music', in Cliff Eisen and Alan Davison (eds.), *Late Eighteenth-Century Music and
Visual Culture* (Turnhout: Brepols, 2017), pp. 155–72, 162.

[104] See Richard Macksey, 'Foreword', in Gérard Genette, *Paratexts: Thresholds of Interpretation*
(New York: Cambridge University Press, 1997), xviii: The paratext comprises 'those liminal
devices and conventions, both within the book (*peritext*) and outside it (*epitext*), that mediate
the book to the reader: titles and subtitles, pseudonyms, forewords, dedications, epigraphs,

market Mozart's music spans his entire composing career, and extends well beyond it. But their function in the process of canon formation becomes more obvious in posthumous editions (i.e., after 1791). Decorative title pages bear indications of the status of arrangements and arrangers around 1800: the fact that the contents have been arranged, and sometimes the name of the arranger, are often announced with pride. At this stage there is no sense that the arrangement is less than, or even separate from, the principal text or musical work.

Title pages for late eighteenth-century music editions, including those of Mozart's music, typically set out four textual elements in a hierarchical order: main title (specific, generic, occasionally both); performing forces; name of composer(s), and sometimes arranger; and publisher/place of sale. Regrettably the date is usually not given. Additional elements that might be present include a subtitle, dedication, opus number (or the equivalent), publication registration details, the price, and the name of the engraver. Occasionally there is information about possible performance practices, or statements about the authority of the musical text. The language of the title page did not necessarily reflect the place of publication: Latin, Italian, and French were used internationally, while English and Germanic languages imply local distribution.[105] Andrea Klitzing notes particular conventions regarding the language used on title pages of arrangements that were tied up with German nationalism. For piano reductions of Mozart's operas, German or Italian was used almost exclusively, but after 1818 the number of German title pages for such arrangements increases significantly.[106]

Artaria published many of the editions of works by Haydn and Mozart that appeared during their lifetimes, but the many other German publishing houses that flourished in the late eighteenth century also established their names through their editions of these composers' works. These publishers got away with this in the era before copyright by producing new arrangements, and could boost their sales by using enticing title pages to draw the reader in. For one of their first publications, for example, Simrock in Bonn chose to issue what is one of the earliest piano scores of *Die Zauberflöte* (1793), with a title page adorned with a specifically designed engraving by Johann Gottfried Pflugfelder (Figure 5). Like the opera, the title page is loaded with symbols that would have had a quite particular meaning for Freemasons in Mozart's Vienna. Along

---

prefaces, intertitles, notes, epilogues, and afterwords'. On the dedication as paratext, see Emily H. Green (ed.), *Dedicating Music, 1785–1850* (Rochester, NY: University of Rochester Press, 2019), chapters 1–4.

[105] David Wyn Jones, 'What Do Surviving Copies of Early Printed Music Tell Us?', in *Music Publishing in Europe 1600–1900*, pp. 139–58, 145.

[106] Andrea Klitzing, *Don Giovanni unter Druck: Die Verbreitung der Mozart-Oper als instrumentale Kammermusik im deutschsprachigen Raum bis 1850*, Abhandlungen zur Musikgeschichte (Göttingen: V&R Unipress, 2020), p. 257.

Figure 5 Simrock's piano score of *Die Zauberflöte*, title page engraving by Johann Gottfried Pflugfelder, Bonn, 1793. Image © Karin Breitner, ed., *Katalog der Sammlung Anthony van Hoboken in der Musiksammlung der Österreichischen Nationalbibliothek*

with the urn and pyramid, and Papageno's pipes, this illustration shows the Egyptian High Priestess, veiled Isis, in the foreground. Isis was a favourite statuary image in the late eighteenth-century garden, symbolising the mysteries of nature; she was also a primary icon in Masonic rituals of the late eighteenth century. In *Die Zauberflöte* she represents the end of Tamino's initiation process. Beneath her veil all the mysteries and the knowledge of the past were said to be hidden. The act of pulling back her veil – or perhaps, by extension, turning the pages of Simrock's edition – was thought to represent a step towards enlightenment, and ultimately towards immortality.

According to Genette's analysis, the importance of a paratextual element is defined as much by the 'sender' (usually here the publisher and editor) as by the 'addressee' (here the music amateur or professional).[107] Paratextual messages may be also understood as official or unofficial, overt or covert.[108] For Nikolaus Simrock in turn-of-the-nineteenth-century Bonn, there would have been personal as well as professional benefits in promoting *Die Zauberflöte*'s enlightenment message through a carefully chosen title page. He was himself a member of a group of enlightenment thinkers, the *Illuminatenorden*, and a founding member

---

[107] Genette, *Paratexts: Thresholds of Interpretation*, pp. 8–9.   [108] Ibid., pp. 9–10.

of a related reading group; and in 1805 he founded a Masonic lodge, *Les frères courageux*. But the title page speaks not only of Mozart, masonry, and Simrock, but also of arranger Friedrich Eunike (1764–1844), composer and opera singer, whose name appears as prominently as that of Simrock. Born in Sachsenhausen on March 6, 1764, he received his first music lessons from his father. In 1786, his tenor voice earned him a call to Schwedt as a Margravial chamber singer. He toured Germany and Amsterdam, finding great acclaim, and was also active as a composer. His 1792 piano reduction of *Die Zauberflöte* was published in Darmstadt by Boßler, and several of his songs appeared in print. His reputation would have profited from this arrangement, and also helped to give the arrangement a certain authority.

Lithographic editions allowed the printing of more lavish and detailed title pages, as well as more copies than engraving.[109] The publisher André from Offenbach was an early champion of new lithographic techniques for music publication from 1800, and was an important publisher of Mozart's music. The first work to be printed using lithography in its more advanced form was a set of string parts for an arrangement of Mozart's *Die Zauberflöte*, in 1797 or 1798.[110] In some cases a mixture of methods was used to create an edition of music; for example, around 1805 Johann August Böhme in Hamburg produced an engraved piano score of *Così fan tutte* with a lithographed title-page vignette.[111] A magnificent example of a fully lithographed edition is Maurice Schlesinger's 1822 piano score of *Così*, with a title-page vignette (Figure 6). This edition, and the Simrock publication just mentioned, are unusual for German editions in that the artists of the vignettes are identified.[112]

Exceptional in its decorative title page, this edition was typical in its musical contents. Most opera-related publications were piano reductions, destined for private performance in the home. There was, however, a steadily growing demand for full scores.

Gottfried Fraenkel claims that the more ornate title pages of nineteenth-century music are found predominantly in sheet music of songs and dances, whereas few publishers of 'serious music' gave consideration to decoration.[113] Yet elaborate title pages, including those with specifically

---

[109] Lithographic technique entails writing back-to-front on polished stone with fatted ink; the printer's ink is rolled over the wet stone, and sticks to the fatty marks while being repelled everywhere else by the water.

[110] A. Beverly Barksdale, ed., *The Printed Note: 500 Years of Music Printing and Engraving* (New York: Da Capo Press, 1981), p. 122.

[111] For further details, see Karin Breitner, *Katalog der Sammlung Anthony van Hoboken in der Musiksammlung der Österreichischen Nationalbibliothek*, vol. 12, *Wolfgang Amadeus Mozart, Werke KV 585–626a* (Tutzing: Schneider, 1993), p. 4.

[112] Other notable exceptions include the signed Haydn and Mozart title pages dating from the beginning of the nineteenth century, issued by Breitkopf and Härtel.

[113] Gottfried S. Fraenkel, *Decorative Title Pages: 201 Examples from 1500 to 1800* (New York: Dover, 1968), p. 3.

Figure 6 Schlesinger's publication of the piano score of *Così fan Tutte* with title page vignette, Paris, 1822. Image © Karin Breitner, ed., *Katalog der Sammlung Anthony van Hoboken in der Musiksammlung der Österreichischen Nationalbibliothek*

designed vignettes, were clearly also associated with editions of the latter kind: they could be designed to lend weight to these publications, perhaps particularly those in the form of arrangements, helping the buyer to view them as 'timeless' documents, monuments to great composers and their works. Thus it seems clear that these arrangements were not understood – or marketed – as 'poor relations' of the original works. On the contrary, publishers used nicely packaged arrangements to facilitate the process of canonising their chosen works and composers.

The iconography and typography that we find on early title pages for Mozart's music were used to elevate particular genres, and to capitalise on their success. Title pages for Mozart's piano concertos – some of the most popular and best known of his works in his lifetime – are good hunting grounds for canonising imagery. According to David Wyn Jones, it was the lack of these works, in particular, in the late eighteenth-century London market for published music that delayed the reception of Mozart as musical genius by English audiences.[114] But the reception of Mozart there was soon to be boosted as regards another genre: in London from around 1811, a new and intense interest in Mozart was inspired by performances of his operas at the King's Theatre. Early nineteenth-century English publishers of arrangements of Mozart's operas drew on and contributed to this late-blooming enthusiasm for Mozart in England.[115]

Around 1819–20, the London publisher Goulding D'Almaine, Potter, and Co., together with editor Joseph Mazzinghi, who had been musical director of the King's Theatre since 1784, launched a series of engraved editions of arrangements of Mozart's operas, each with detailed dedicated title-page vignettes.[116] The five vignettes that adorned the first five of these editions were probably the work of stipple engraver James Hopwood (c.1752–1819). Like some of the earlier German title pages for Mozart opera, they show particular scenes in the operas, and, according to Hyatt King, were based on sketches made during rehearsals or even actual performances.[117] Favourite pivotal scenes were chosen, such as the moment in Act 1, Scene 7 of *Le nozze di Figaro* when Count Almaviva lifts a dress that has been placed over a chair to reveal Cherubino hiding underneath, much to the horror of Suzanna and the amusement of Don Basilio. Hopwood's engraving from *Don Giovanni* is drawn from Act 2, Scene 15: the moment in which the Don has refused the Commendatore's last offer of a chance to repent (see Figure 4). As Hyatt King observes, these lively little pictures would have helped potential purchasers to recall scenes, and perhaps music, from the operas.[118]

Thus title pages could open enticing windows on a work, which made them ideal for publisher's displays. There is a connection to be made here between these illustrated title pages (especially prominent in nineteenth-century Mozart opera arrangements), and their contents, the arrangements themselves. Both

[114] David Wyn Jones, 'From Artaria to Longman & Broderip: Mozart's Music on Sale in London', in David Wyn Jones and Otto Biba (eds.), *Studies in Music History Presented to H.C. Robbins Landon on His Seventieth Birthday* (London: Thames & Hudson, 1996), pp. 105–14, 110–11.

[115] For a detailed discussion, see Alec Hyatt King, 'Vignettes in Early Nineteenth-Century London Editions of Mozart's Operas', *British Library Journal* 6/1 (1986), pp. 24–43.

[116] On Mozart arrangements as a source for Mozart reception history around this time, see Karl Gustav Fellerer, 'Zur Rezeption von Mozarts Opern um die Wende des 18./19. Jahrhunderts', *Mozart-Jahrbuch* 14 (1965), pp. 39–49.

[117] Hyatt King, 'Vignettes in Early Nineteenth-Century London Editions', p. 30.   [118] Ibid.

Figure 7 Title page of André's piano reduction of Mozart's Singspiel *Zaïde*, K. 336b (344), Offenbach, 1838. Image © Karin Breitner, ed., *Katalog der Sammlung Anthony van Hoboken in der Musiksammlung der Österreichischen Nationalbibliothek*

served as appealing reminders of a larger, staged production, asking the amateur reader not only to remember, but also to imaginatively fill in the gaps.

More generally, early title pages for Mozart's operas offer a rich field for the study of canon formation. A slightly later lithographed German edition of Mozart's Singspiel *Zaïde*, K. 336b (344) by André (1838), again a piano reduction, shows more clearly the role that title-page iconography could play in the nineteenth-century canonisation of Mozart. Like the London publications of Mozart opera arrangements, this edition also capitalises on the success of Mozart's operas by this time, and in a highly effective way. It figuratively engraves Mozart's name and the names of nine of his operas on the reader's visual memory, in that the display type used to print Mozart's name, the largest element of the title page, is itself inscribed with the titles of nine of his operas: *Die Entführung aus dem Serail*, *Idomeneo*, *Le nozze di Figaro*, *Der Schauspieldirektor*, *Die Zauberflöte*, *Così fan tutte*, *Zaïde* itself, *La clemenza di Tito* ('*Titus*'), and *Don Giovanni* respectively (Figure 7). Such typographic tricks – titles within titles – were typical of a market-savvy publisher like André; but they were also used by many other publishers when they listed on title pages other arrangements they had available in their stock. The subtitle 'Klavierauszug' (piano reduction) is prominently and proudly proclaimed in drop-shadow capital letters, creating a three-dimensional effect.

We can understand these graphic elements using Genette's conception of the paratext: 'More than a boundary or a sealed border,' writes Genette, the paratext is 'a *threshold* . . . a zone not only of transition but also of *transaction*'.[119] With what he terms the 'illocutionary force of its message', the paratext could invoke a commitment with the weight of a promise on the part of the publisher (acting partly on behalf of the author).[120] Several of these early Mozart title pages clearly promulgated the idea of the composer, his works, and the printed musical texts within the editions as monumental, fixed, and sacrosanct entities. So it may surprise today's musicians to find that the contents of some of these editions are actually arrangements, not full orchestral versions or the original instrumentation. But contemporary users perceived no contradiction. Eyebrows were only raised when, in a few exceptional cases, publishers tried to pass off arrangements as original works. Otherwise the designation 'arrangement' on the title page around 1800 can be understood more as an enticement to purchase than a detraction, as offering something more rather than less than the full score: more accessible, more fun, more educational, more geared to developing one's own imagination.

5 Arrangement History around 1850: Losing Touch

In his 1865 revised version of Koch's *Lexicon*, Arrey von Dommer had quite a lot more than Koch (cited in part 1) to say about musical arrangement, and in a newly polemical tone:

> Arrangement means reconfiguring a piece of music for other voices or instruments than [those] for which it was originally set. Thus, for example, orchestral works for piano, two-handed or four-handed, or for string quartet, for individual string and wind instruments, or only for wind instruments. For a skilled arranger of the craft and a speculative publisher, it is not easy to find a piece of music that cannot be arranged for any instrument, even if it were the Ninth Symphony for flute and drum. One has also stooped to the stupidity of arranging solo piano pieces of the most pianistic nature, such as Beethoven sonatas, or, to push the nonsense even higher, Bach organ toccatas, for orchestra. Nevertheless, such experiments are still harmless in comparison to the preludes from the Well Temp. Clavier by [J.] S. Bach, arranged by patching in an obbligato cello part, 'added', of course, in the most modern way, and in another arrangement adding in a second concerting [melody-carrying] piano. And not merely with the innocent effort to meet a long-felt need, but with the expressed intention of giving the preludes character, modern colouration, concertante effect; cf. Moscheles, Studies in Melodious Counterpoint etc., Op. 137 *a, b*. A shining example of artistic understanding and reverence for the masterpieces.[121]

---

[119] Genette, *Paratexts*, pp. 1–2 (italics original).   [120] Ibid., pp. 10–11.

[121] Arrey von Dommer, *Musikalisches Lexicon. Auf der Grundlage des Lexicon's von H. Ch. Koch* (Heidelberg: Academische Verlagsbuchhandlung von J. C. B. Mohr, 1865), pp. 67–8 (italics original), https://books.google.co.nz/books?id=uF_0AAAAMAAJ&printsec=frontcover.

This extended definition indicates the ways arrangements had diversified and changed by the mid-nineteenth century, and their increasingly problematic status. Dommer uses the definition as an opportunity for a polemical account of what can happen to the musical work (especially certain canonical works) when its meaning is disrupted by arrangers with extreme ambitions. In Dommer's time – which overlapped the age of musical copyright, regular concert performance, and widening dissemination of music – musical arrangement should no longer be taken for granted as necessary, or interpreted broadly and pragmatically. Now there were agreed right and wrong ways of carrying out arrangements, regarding both the original and the destination works. Around 1800 Koch remarked on the arranging of 'entire operas' for wind instruments 'or even' as quartets. In 1865, Dommer makes no mention of opera, but rather cites instrumental music; and as for destination genres, piano arrangements are mentioned first. The canonising functions of arrangement are clearly spelled out, preceding this complaining part of the definition. By this time, arrangements celebrate 'masterworks' by making them larger, grander, or otherwise more 'masterful'; they might still be scaled down (which Koch had emphasised), but certainly not trivialised.

Dommer's discussion of arrangement gets tied up with nationalism – the symphonic heritage and masterworks, especially of Beethoven, are perceived as 'protected'. Bach's instrumental works (the Well-Tempered Clavier, the organ toccatas), in particular, cannot be taken in vain – as in rearranged out of their idiomatic original form. But what is really being protected here is an emerging German cultural lineage, arising from its great composers and prized works of the past. This explains why German instrumental music is foregrounded in Dommer's definition, even though, as we shall see, there were plenty of arrangements of operas, and not just those of Mozart. This protection comes with a trade-off, which I will discuss below under the heading of 'losing touch'. I consider how the culture of musical arrangement changed with the understanding of musical works during the late eighteenth and nineteenth centuries, looking at what happens to arrangements of Haydn's symphonies and Mozart's operas in particular.

Meeting the Market, or Representing the Original?

How arrangements of Haydn's symphonies and Mozart's operas changed over the nineteenth century is such a large topic that it can only be touched upon here. Arrangers' approaches to the task of converting a symphony or opera to chamber music raise two immediate questions: to what extent arrangers tried to respect the original work and account for all its timbres and textures; and to what extent they catered to the changing and growing market of musicians who purchased and performed them. It is easy to assume that the strongest pull on the arranger was that of the market. But composers exerted authority over their works even before the era of copyright, and concern for fidelity to the original text in both publication and performance was growing during the nineteenth century. In Haydn's day, arrangers like Salomon and Clementi met and worked alongside Haydn as colleagues. As such, they had something to gain by producing arrangements that would give performers a good sense of the original, while juggling consideration for the needs of amateurs in the home.

Regarding opera arrangements, the waters were muddier from the outset in terms of what exactly constituted the 'work' and what the 'arrangement' – and who did what in terms of composition and arrangement. Composing operas was an altogether more collaborative affair than composing instrumental music, in that there was always a librettist, and sometimes more than one composer (in the case of pastiche operas for example).[122] Operas were subject to repeated rearrangement by their composers, to cater to local traditions and particular singers; and opera composers often had a hand in creating piano reductions, which frequently appeared early in the works' publication history.

There are some broad trends in the way arrangers juggled the sometimes conflicting imperatives of fidelity to the original work and manageable chamber music for amateurs through the late eighteenth and nineteenth centuries. Early on, the arrangers clearly seek to cater to amateurs in a flexible way. Thus much detail is omitted in the trio transcriptions by Salomon of Haydn's London symphonies (1798), including, for example, the horn calls that enrich the texture at the end of the slow movement from Symphony No. 104. In the quintet version, Salomon is able to add in these horn calls as double stops in the viola (see Example 6). In the later Clementi version (1816), the piano is no longer marked 'ad libitum', but is an integral part of the texture and could even be played alone; but even there the horn calls are not integrated (Example 7). Later transcribers, like Hummel and Liszt, were more concerned to pack as much as possible into the piano, where it appeared as the central ensemble member in a chamber arrangement. Hummel arranged Haydn's Symphonies Nos. 22 in E minor and 100 in G major for his favoured ensemble: piano, flute, violin, and cello.

This flexible catering to amateurs' needs applies even more to opera arrangements around 1800. Indeed, throughout the late eighteenth and nineteenth centuries operas were treated much more flexibly than instrumental works. There is much more of a culture of excerpting, rearranging, even recomposing – and the range of possible arrangement types is correspondingly larger – to create many different versions, tailored to difference places and people. But there is a tendency to arrange operas in their entirety after 1800, especially after 1815.

---

[122] On pastiche operas being prized in eighteenth-century England, see Alison C. Desimone, *The Power of Pastiche: Musical Miscellany and Cultural Identity in Early Eighteenth-Century England* (Liverpool: Liverpool University Press, 2021).

Die Entführung, *Don Giovanni*, *Così*, and *Die Zauberflöte*. But Ulrich also arranged operas by Auber, Bellini, Boieldieu, Cimarosa, Donizetti, Gluck, Herold, Méhul, Paër, Reissiger, Rossini, Spontini, and Weber – in other words, well-known opera composers of the late eighteenth and nineteenth centuries, mostly of Italian opera.

Several features of Ulrich's translation of Haydn's Symphony No. 104 make it very amenable to amateur performers in the home: he reduces textures so that the hands of each player are not given something complex and different at once; he uses dynamics, rather than chord density and extremely thick textures, to achieve weightiness; and he uses the high register strategically, just to highlight particular effects. In the second movement of Symphony No. 104, for example, the texture becomes thick and complex as the second section begins and strings alternate with winds. But Ulrich simplifies these textures and divides string and wind writing between the two players (see Example 8). Likewise in the complexly layered overture to *Don Giovanni*, Ulrich separates the roles between the players in his transcription, while retaining elements of the musical sublime that foreshadow the finale. Secondo has low-register tremolo, and thick chords; Primo takes care of syncopation and chromaticism (Example 9).

As the quotation from Dommer's revised edition of Koch's *Lexicon* suggests, there was a pronounced trend of increasing insistence on piano works, and especially four-hand piano. Adolph Hofmeister's catalogues of published music appeared regularly throughout the nineteenth century – the third edition of 1844 lists close to 9,000 individual publications of four-hand piano music. Hofmeister lists publications appearing only in Germany and its 'neighbouring lands'. Were we to add to Hofmeister's list the catalogues of contemporary English, French, and Italian publishers, the number of works would be much larger.

What kinds of music were arranged for piano duet? As in the arrangements by Ulrich, we find that opera arrangements are particularly popular, and Mozart's name figures prominently. Of the sixty-eight publications of works by Mozart listed in arrangements for four-hand piano, fourteen relate to his operas, and only one to a symphony. But elsewhere in the catalogue orchestral music is very well represented in the arrangements for piano four-hands, especially the later symphonies of Haydn (see Table 8). Note that the keys indicate a reverse ordering of most of the twelve London symphonies in the first three of these lists (Nos. 104 in D major through to No. 93, also in D major). The naming of arrangers and the substantial collected editions of arrangers are also later nineteenth-century trends, both of which helped popularise these works.

Although Hanslick observed that arrangements for string quartet were being replaced by four-hand arrangements (see Section 4), string quartet and string quintet arrangements still enjoyed some popularity in his day. Dommer

Example 8 (a) Arrangement of Haydn's Symphony No. 104, second movement, bars 38–44, for piano four hands, by Hugo Ulrich (Leipzig: C. F. Peter, c.1870); (b) Haydn's Symphony No. 104, second movement, bars 38–44, orchestral original

mentions arrangements for string quartet next after those for piano. Of the twenty-five quintet items listed in Hofmeister's 1844 catalogue under 'Mozart', nine are arrangements, four of which are opera arrangements. Looking more closely at these lists, one can see a growth in music publishing in the early nineteenth century in two areas: scores and collections. These forms received a decisive boost as early as 1801, when Pleyel published the *Collection complète des quatuors d'Haydn, dediée au Premier Consul Bonaparte*. Then, in 1802, Pleyel started to release the first miniature scores, *Bibliothèque musicale*, with an edition of four of Haydn's symphonies; then came ten editions, between them containing his string quartets.[125]

125 See Benton, Rita, s.v. 'Pleyel (i), Ignace Joseph Pleyel, §1: Life', *Oxford Music Online*, www-oxfordmusiconline-com.ezproxy.auckland.ac.nz/grovemusic/view/10.1093/gmo/9781561592630.001.0001/.

Example 9 Arrangement of Mozart's *Don Giovanni*, K. 527, Overture bars 1–18, for piano four hands, by Hugo Ulrich (Leipzig: C. F. Peter, c.1870)

The publication of scores gave listeners an overview of works that only piano reductions had previously afforded. The increasing publication of scores of various types during the nineteenth century (starting with the higher-status genres like symphonies and string chamber music) meant that scores tended to take over some of the earlier functions of arrangements, especially those of

Example 9 (cont.)

education and *Bildung*. Collections of works also became more popular. Of the forty-nine quartets listed in the 1844 Hofmeister catalogue under 'Mozart', three items are sets of scores, and one of these, 'Collection des quartets ou partitions', includes arrangements. This was unusual for the time: the late nineteenth century was the era of collections of celebrated works, only originals, with arrangements explicitly excluded. Titles like '10 Quatuors

Table 8 Haydn symphonies arranged for piano four-hands in Hofmeister/Whistling catalogue of 1844 ('Sonaten etc. für das Pianoforte zu vier Händen', pp. 86 and 99)

Haydn, 13 Symphonien, arr. v. Brissler.
No. 1 in D. No. 2, in Es. No. 3, in B. No. 4, in G. No. 5, in Es. No. 6, in D. No. 7, in G (mit dem Paukenschlage). No. 8, in D. No. 9, in C. No. 10 (La Reine) in B. No. 11 (périodique) in D. No. 12 (périodique) in Gm. No. 13, (Op. 77, No. 1) in Cm. No. 14, (Op. 77, No. 2) in D. No.15 (Op. 66, No. 3) in Es. No. 16, (Op. 56, No. 2) in G. Berlin, Challer u. C. à 1 R.

Haydn, 14 Symphonien, arr. v. Klage.
No. 1, in D. No. 2, in Es. No. 3 in B. No. 4, in G. No. 5, in Es. No. 6 in D. No. 7, in G (mit dem Paukenschlag). No. 8, in D. No. 9, in C. No. 10, in B (La Reine). No. 11, in D. No. 12, in Gm. No. 13, in Cm. No. 14, in C (L'Ours). Berlin, Krigar à 1 R 5 N.

Haydn, Sinfonies, arr. p. F. Mockwitz.
No. 1, in D. No. 2, in Es. No. 3, in B. No. 4, in G. No. 5, in Es. No. 6, in D. No. 7 in G (mit dem Paukenschlag). No. 8, in D. No. 9, in C. Berlin, Riefenstahl à 1 R 5 N.

Haydn, Sinfonie, arr.
in Gm. [No. 39] (Oeuvres arr. No. 2) Zürich, Nägeli 1 R 5 N.

Haydn, Sinfonie, arr. p. Reim.
No. 1, in G. No. 2, in D. Berlin, Schlesinger à 1 R 10 N.

Haydn, Sinfonie, arr. p. Stegmann.
No. 1, in Dm. No. 2, B. No. 3, in Cm. No. 4, in D. No. 5 (Militaire), in G. Bonn, Simrock à 4 f.

Haydn, Sinfonie mit d. Paukenwirbel arr.
(in Es) [No. 103] Hamb. Cranz 1 R 10 N.

Haydn, Sinf., arr. p. Hoffmann
(in Es.) [No. 103] Offenb. André 2 f.

Originaux' and '10 Principaux Quatuors' suggest that publishers assigned to the original quartets a different genre status from the arrangements. Nonetheless, in Hofmeister twenty-two arrangements are listed at the end of the Mozart quartets category, and twenty of them are opera arrangements, some in several versions (for example, there are four different versions of *Die Zauberflöte*). This suggests that the string quartet remained popular as a medium for arrangements, as did opera arrangements in general.

Other trends from the early nineteenth century also continued. Arrangements for string instruments, which had been so popular in the first part of the nineteenth century, persisted even while piano transcriptions now took centre stage. The quartet arrangements were still played mostly by men, the piano transcriptions often by women. String quartet parties still sought to develop the performer and to foster *Bildung*. And the focus in domestic piano (ensemble) performance was (still) often on displaying the (female) performer to best advantage, that is, exhibiting just the right amount of *Bildung*. An example of arrangement probably targeted at women is August Reinhard's trio arrangement of the Adagio and Allegro from Haydn's Symphony No. 104 ('London'), for cello, harmonium, and piano (alternatively violin and piano), which appears in a set from circa 1900. Reinhard chose to excerpt mostly slow movements in this series, which speaks to the prevailing reverence for 'works of Classical and modern masters' as they are described on the title page – Germans of the Late Baroque and Classical era: Handel, Mozart, and Beethoven – which the publisher and arranger were evidently seeking to promote (Figure 8).[126] It also speaks to the intended performers: arrangements of slow movements would be within the reach of amateurs; and female performers (here on piano, harmonium, or both) could be expected to enact or even embody the piety, sensibility, and reverence that these movements, their composers, and the 'Classical' era in general were now thought to demand. Ulrich's publisher, Peters, also joined in this canon-forming process: the title pages enshrine Haydn's London symphonies with the Classical façade, angels, and wreaths.

Arrangements and the Concept of the Musical Work

> Arrangement, then, will essentially be for us the paradigm of a critical, active relationship with works.[127]

As Peter Szendy has noted, the idea of arrangements – what they are, what they do – is tied up with the development of the concept of 'musical works'. Szendy finds a crucial 'moment' in this history in the mid-nineteenth century, especially

---

[126] See Margaret Notley, 'Late Nineteenth-Century Chamber Music and the Cult of the Classical Adagio', *19th-Century Music* 23/1 (1999), pp. 33–61.

[127] Szendy, *Listen*, p. 39.

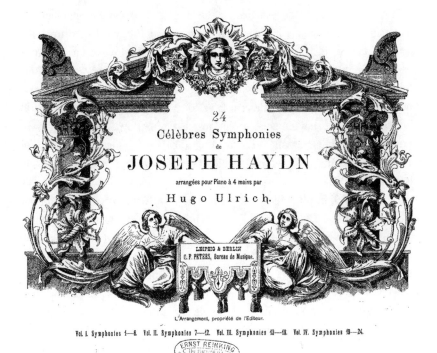

Figure 8 Title page of Ulrich's arrangement of Haydn's Symphony No. 104
('London') (Leipzig: C. F. Peters, c.1870)

in the thinking about arrangements of Schumann and Liszt. At this time there is
a Romantic understanding of musical works as artworks that are forever sought
but never attained. This aspect of Romanticism can be understood by reference to
the idea of the fragment, an emblem of Romanticism around 1800, theorised by
German writers associated with the Jena School, especially in the journal *The
Athenaeum* (1798–1800). For these writers, the fragment is a quintessentially
Romantic phenomenon because it leaves much room for the free play of the
imagination, and a perpetual play of possible completions in the mind of the
beholder, reader, or listener.[128] Early proponents of musical Romanticism understood Romantic musical works similarly: they are forever in process (*im Werden*).
Szendy observes that this processual character is even clearer in arrangements,
which can leave performers and listeners much room for imaginative completions. So arrangements could exist in parallel and on a par with original versions
of Romantic works, each gesturing towards the unattainable work. Szendy argues

---

[128] For relevant discussions of the Romantic fragment, see my *Beethoven's Theatrical Quartets,
Opp. 59, 74 and 95* (Cambridge: Cambridge University Press, 2013), pp. 206–8.

that in Schumann or Liszt, especially, 'the original and the arrangement are complementary, contiguous in their incompleteness and their distance from the essence of the work'.[129] Szendy labels arrangements that invoke this sense of reaching towards but not attaining the musical work 'Romantic arrangements'.[130]

Such Romantic arrangements are quite particular, in their flexible (and pluralistic) elaboration of a musical idea. Szendy points to Liszt's 'ossia' indications in his arrangements, directions that provide performers with an alternative for a given passage. Liszt is exceptional among arrangers in writing in these options, thus offering explicit flexibility in how one realises the work: 'Liszt . . . did indeed "canonize" the Pastoral [in his transcription of Beethoven's Sixth Symphony], but he did this by revealing in it, with his *ossia*, an unsuspected mobility'.[131] But this flexible conception, Szendy finds, has been lost. The idea of Romantic arrangement fades almost as soon as it arises, with the countervailing rise of the musical 'work-concept'. This conception of the musical work is based on the idea – common in today's scholarship, analysis, and performance of Western Classical music – that composers produce original works (Urtexte) that are essentially complete at the time of composition (in the 'Fassung letzter Hand', roughly 'definitive version'). So the musical work came to be thought necessarily prior to, more authoritative than, and thus superior to any arrangement; and arrangements came to be considered lesser derivatives.[132]

Szendy's theory of the 'Romantic arrangement' and its 'moment' is useful especially regarding Liszt, Schumann, Berlioz, and certain of their contemporaries' *ideals*. But it does not offer a complete or compelling picture of their *practices*. Szendy finds that arrangers like Schumann and Liszt take us close to how they personally want to hear the original works in question: they are 'remarkable listeners who sign and write down their listenings'.[133] That is, if we listen to Liszt's *Fantasie über Themen aus Mozarts Figaro und Don Giovanni* (*Fantasy on Themes form Mozart's Figaro and Don Giovanni*, 1842), or indeed his transcription for two pianos of Beethoven's Ninth Symphony (1850), we apparently gain insights into how Liszt actually heard those works. But this argument runs the risk of the intentional fallacy (the problem of judging an artwork by the intent or purpose of its artist, generally agreed to be ultimately unknowable), and it also raises the problem of treating listening as historically invariant.

These 'listenings' that Liszt and others offer us through their arrangements are not necessarily just ways of imparting how they listened. They might also be ways of telling us what to listen for, or how we ought to listen to the works in

[129] Szendy, *Listen*, p. 38.   [130] Ibid., p. 39.   [131] Ibid., p. 59.   [132] Ibid., pp. 48–9.
[133] Ibid., p. 39.

question; their function can be normative, clarifying, or corrective, and they certainly play a major role in canon formation.[134] Arrangements with a 'corrective' function might be understood as resembling certain works by mid- to late nineteenth-century visual artists, which by depicting silent, reverent listening, implicitly show us *how to* listen, rather than (or as well as) how *they* listen.[135] Indeed some of these arrangements circa 1850 might be precisely geared to preparing listeners to listen attentively to 'Masterworks' in the concert hall. In this sense, such arrangements align with and reinforce the emerging concept of the work in the nineteenth century.

There are further points to be made against stressing the 'Romantic arrangement' and its 'moment'. One concerns the tendency around 1830 to publish piano reductions of operas *'ohne Worte'* (without words). This trend might initially have been related straightforwardly to Romanticism, in the sense discussed by Szendy. So, *'ohne Worte'* arrangements might be understood as independent and dramatically valid instances of a given work, which point towards a particular yet-to-be-realised work, thus calling upon the performer and listener to 'complete' the work in various ways. An even more telling sign of the 'moment' of Romantic arrangements might be the tendency of publishers to drop the designation *'ohne Worte'* from title pages, as the practice of omitting the words became common in the nineteenth century: the piano reduction was freed to become a vehicle (perhaps *the* vehicle in Liszt's opinion) for arrangements that left room for performers and listeners to find their own imaginative routes towards the work.

But Klitzing warns against this interpretation of *'ohne Worte'* arrangements, preferring a more pragmatic view. These arrangements appeared during a rapid internationalisation of publishing. On the one hand, German publishers tried to advertise arrangements of German music as national cultural products by using German on title pages, where once French and Italian were often seen (*'senza Parole'* and so on), especially after the 1815 Congress of Vienna. On the other hand, German music publishers sought a more international market with their editions, so that opera piano reductions with no words (as indicated on the title page, or tacitly presumed) catered to a broad European audience, especially after the 1829 formation of the Leipzig cartel of music publishers against reprinting.[136] So the many editions of opera arrangements *'ohne Worte'* arguably have more to do with the market situation than Romantic idealism.

In practice, too, the relationship of arrangement to 'work' is more complex than Szendy's 'moment' implies. Exactly when the concept of the musical work

---

[134] Ibid., p. 43.   [135] See my *Cultivating String Quartets in Beethoven's Vienna*, pp. 190–4.
[136] Klitzing, *Don Giovanni unter Druck*, p. 235.

crystalised and became regulative is still debated among scholars. Lydia Goehr dates it around 1800 and sees Beethoven's symphonies as paradigmatic of its development.[137] Harry White dates the concept of the work earlier, back to the time of Bach at least.[138] For Szendy it crystallises later, around the time of Schumann and Liszt in the mid-nineteenth century. But Szendy also notes that key related concepts developed earlier, and at different times in different places. In Germany in particular, Englishman Charles Burney encountered the idea of fidelity to the original in performance at the Prussian court in 1777, implying a conception of musical works as full and complete originals.[139] In Versailles in the time of Les 24 Violons du Roi (1626–1761) an ideal of the perfect performance also operated.[140] This arguably implies a concept of fidelity to the original work, and correspondingly downplays arrangements as unfaithful or imperfect derivatives.

Szendy makes an exception for Italy, as a late-comer to the 'work-concept', because of the prevalence of opera there and the fluid concept of the work it entailed. But opera, and the fundamental understanding or ontology of the work that was particular to it, represents more than an exception: it arguably exerts a Europe-wide force in opposition to 'work-concept thinking' into the late nineteenth century, even as the work-concept was championed by influential advocates like Hanslick. Opera and its peculiar ontology infiltrated all aspects of musical life in the main centres of musical activity (including homes) in late eighteenth- and nineteenth-century Europe. This is nicely demonstrated in Traeg's catalogue, where, as we saw in Section 1, opera in various arrangements permeates all categories, and messes up any efforts to impose a tidy classification by genre, or by 'place' (church/theatre/chamber), on musical items. The work-concept developed in opposition to opera and all that it stood for ontologically – especially as arrangement, so crucial to promulgation of an operatic work, became distinguished as a separate and supposedly lesser activity from 'original composition'. But composers across Europe in the era of Mozart, Haydn, and Beethoven were arguably influenced more by the special character of opera – its popularity and associated job security, its aesthetics, and its collaborative nature – than by anything else in musical culture at the time.

In sum, rather than defining a 'moment' of the 'Romantic arrangement', which gives way to a regulative concept of the musical work in the mid-nineteenth

---

[137] Goehr, *The Imaginary Museum of Musical Works*.

[138] Harry White, '"If It's Baroque, Don't Fix It": Reflections on Lydia Goehr's "Work-Concept" and the Historical Integrity of Musical Composition', *Acta Musicologica* 69/1 (1997), pp. 94–104.

[139] Szendy, *Listen*, p. 40.

[140] John Spitzer and Neal Zaslaw, *The Birth of the Orchestra: History of an Institution (1650–1815)* (Oxford: Oxford University Press, 2004), especially chapter 3 on 'The Lully Myth', pp. 70–2.

century, it would be more useful to define 'arrangement' as something essentially Romantic, and to back-date musical Romanticism into what we continue to call the Classical era (usually 1750–1800). It is pertinent how arrangements interact with an emerging concept of the musical work over a longer period in the late eighteenth and nineteenth centuries, rather in the way that musical styles interact in Friedrich Blume's concept of a 'Classic-Romantic' era.[141] After all, fragments – which are aligned to arrangements in that they leave a role for the receiving subject (viewer or reader) – flourished in the 'Classic-Romantic' era in which this Element is situated. Consider the many paintings of ruins of the late eighteenth and early nineteenth centuries; or the many Romantic poems which were published explicitly *as* 'fragments': Coleridge's *Kubla Khan: or a Vision in a Dream. A Fragment* (1797); Keats's *Hyperion. A Fragment* (1820); Byron's *The Giaour, A Fragment of a Turkish Tale* (1813). The later 'Romantic arrangements' of Liszt and his followers might actually be seen as leading away from 'arrangement thinking' towards 'work-concept thinking', in their insistence on including much of the original composition. In fact Liszt's 'ossia' indications can be taken as enabling different pianists to achieve a high degree of 'completion' of an arranged work, by providing options for them to get as close to original as their technical capabilities will allow.

Losing Touch

In this chapter I have discussed two principal types of arrangement that emerged in the course of the nineteenth century, using a typology based on place (public or private). But the history is more complex than the tidy split into public and private spheres allows. As we have seen with opera arrangements, the type of music (genre) and the composer also had a bearing on how a given work was treated by an arranger. At any one point in the history charted in this Element various types of arrangement coexisted. This complexity grows in the early- to mid-nineteenth century: then there emerged more and various 'public' types of arrangement, such as those of Hummel, Clementi, and Liszt, primarily for performance by virtuosi; and various 'private' types, for private entertainment. The public ones are usually signed; the private ones are often designed specifically for amateurs.

Szendy has nothing much to say about the private types; nor does Dommer, who wishes to dismiss them. As Christensen puts it, there are 'the ubiquitous parlour genres one would expect: Waltzes, galops, marches, fantasies, variations ... Potpourris of opera tunes and the like. But also present are

---

[141] Friedrich Blume, *Classic and Romantic Music: A Comprehensive Survey* (New York: Norton, 1970), p. 7.

a large number of transcriptions of more sober concert repertory'.[142] Then as now, scholars have little time for more 'trivial' categories. But these arrangements were produced in great numbers, and one has to set the popular and popularising opera arrangement repertory alongside the canon-forming effort exerted over the symphonic repertory. Moreover, the arrangements destined for private performance by amateurs included vast numbers of symphonies, and the arrangements of operas helped keep operas in performance and in listener's minds; that is, they contributed to canon formation.

There is no monolithic 'moment', if we take these various arrangements into account, when amateurs gained the space and freedom to exercise their imaginations with repertoire they could not normally play, in the privacy of their own homes. Rather, there is a slow change, with some resistance. Slow because with the loss of these manifold types of arrangements destined for amateur performance in their time, we have lost not the significant 'listenings' of the great ears of the past so much as feelings – or a kind of listening that takes place in embodied, active, hands-on performance. We literally *lose touch*. More than a century after Hanslick and Dommer, Roland Barthes glanced back wistfully to the mid- to late nineteenth century's absorption in the four-hand piano transcription:

> I myself began listening to Beethoven's symphonies only by playing them four hands, with a close friend as enthusiastic about them as I was. But nowadays listening to music is dissociated from its practice: many virtuosos, listeners, *en masse*: but as for practitioners, amateurs – very few.[143]

Resistance to the popularising forms of arrangement, so beloved of the amateurs who drove the market, was particularly strong as an aspect of nationalism. Dommer was writing, after all, in the time of Wagner, who was a terrific force against Italian opera and all that it stood for regarding the conception of the musical work. In Dommer's definition, arrangements of Italian operas, such as those at the very height of popularity around 1800, are not so much unmentioned as unmentionable. Any feature of an arrangement that turns a canonic work into something that resembles one of those unmentionable arrangements – such as colouristic effects (flute and drum) and concertante embellishment (added cello part), or anything that smacks of contemporaneity rather than timelessness – detracts too much from the essential character of the work as Masterpiece. Thus the stable German artistic lineage, and cultural heritage these nineteenth-century writers wanted to claim, is threatened.

---

[142] Christensen, 'Four-Hand Piano Transcriptions', p. 257.

[143] See Roland Barthes, 'The Death of the Author', *Image – Music – Text* (London: Fontana, 1977), pp. 142–8 (italics original).

But these arrangements need to be acknowledged. Once we put the everyday – the everyday people, and their everyday music – back into music history, we have a different story to tell about what happens around 1800, which in most of the literature has so far been focused on public events and lives and the 'stately face' of concert life in particular (following Hanslick).[144] In contrast, this Element has emphasised the cultural history of music from the producer/product to the consumer, and has asked us to consider just what 'arrangement' is and means. We have looked at a broad view of arrangement practice as against the increasingly prominent 'work-concept', in contrast to the tidy historiographies devised around 1800, especially regarding the rise of the concept of the musical work. The shifting types of arrangement show that the early to mid-nineteenth century was a crucial time in the development of canon formation and the conception of musical works. By studying the work of various arrangers in Haydn's Europe, for instance, we can start to build up a sense of how his symphonies might have been championed when concert life was just getting started, how they were understood and interpreted during his lifetime, and how they were canonised immediately thereafter. A study of arrangements from this era has considerable relevance today, not only for scholars but also for performers. Christopher Hogwood observes of early arrangers: 'many of their better-wrought products could easily be taken into the repertoire of today's performers'.[145]

The interest and utility of these arrangements for modern-day performers derives not only from their quality, which can be high. The balance of genres represented among arrangements helps to broaden our understanding of chamber music in the era, including the relative popularity of genres and the tremendous resonance of opera through all aspects of musical life. Repertoire of the Classical era for larger chamber groupings of mixed winds and strings might seem scarce, for instance, until we consider arrangements of operas and ballets. Studying arrangements also gives us insight into the way chamber music related to sociability and education, performance practice (particularly for women pianists), and ideals about listening. The 'big name' arrangers might not actually get closer to the score in a documentary sense; but, as Dommer notes, they update or modernise the arrangements; the results can be understood to indicate the performance and listening practices or ideals of the day. Hummel's Mozart arrangements might take us closer to Hummel's own performance practices (as Mark Kroll would have it),[146] or to the way Hummel wanted us

[144] Hanslick, *Geschichte des Concertwesens in Wien*, xiv–xv; see also Sanna Pederson, 'On the Task of the Music Historian: They Myth of the Symphony after Beethoven', *Repercussions* 2/2 (1993), pp. 5–30.

[145] Hogwood, 'In Praise of Arrangements', p. 83.

[146] Kroll (ed.), *Mozart's 'Haffner' and 'Linz' Symphonies*, vii–viii.

to perform Mozart. They might also take us to his own 'hearing' of Mozart (Szendy would say so), or to the way Hummel wanted us to hear Mozart.

The increasingly wide dissemination of arrangements and their changing functions in the nineteenth and early twentieth centuries is a fascinating topic for future study. One of the better represented composers in the archives of New Zealand libraries – which document musical activity in colonial times – is Haydn. And among the better represented works in the vast collections of musical arrangements are his London symphonies. In New Zealand in the late nineteenth century, arrangements functioned as a fairly obvious reminder of homeland and heritage. But they also helped establish an emerging concert life, as they had earlier in Europe. Philharmonic societies were established in Wellington in 1848, Nelson in 1852, New Plymouth in 1856, and Invercargill in 1864. Nineteenth-century Mozart opera arrangements, also well represented in New Zealand music archives, would have been used by such groups as The Auckland Choral Society, established in 1855; the Canterbury Vocal Union (1860); and choral societies in Wellington (1860) and Dunedin (1863). So European settlers imported an established musical culture, in which symphonies and operas occupied an important place, but not always a public one: domestic music-making provided a congenial and portable mode of access, via musical arrangements.

Cambridge Elements ≡

Elements in Music and Musicians 1750–1850

Simon P. Keefe

University of Sheffield

Simon P. Keefe is James Rossiter Hoyle Chair of Music at the University of Sheffield. He is the author of four books on Mozart, including *Mozart in Vienna: The Final Decade* (Cambridge University Press, 2017) and *Mozart's Requiem: Reception, Work, Completion* (Cambridge University Press, 2012), which won the Marjorie Weston Emerson Award from the Mozart Society of America. He is also the editor of seven volumes for Cambridge University Press, including *Mozart Studies* and *Mozart Studies 2*. In 2005 he was elected a life member of the Academy for Mozart Research at the International Mozart Foundation in Salzburg.

About the Series

Music and Musicians, 1750–1850 explores musical culture in the late eighteenth and early nineteenth centuries through individual, cutting-edge studies (c. 30,000 words) that imaginatively re-think a period traditionally associated with high classicism and early romanticism. The series interrogates images and reputations, composers, instruments and performers, critical and aesthetic ideas, travel and migration, and music and social upheaval (including wars and conflicts), thereby demonstrating the cultural vibrancy of the period. Through discussion of musicians' interactions with one another and with non-musicians, real-world experiences in and outside music, evolving reputations, and little studied career contexts and environments, Music and Musicians, 1750–1850 works across the conventional 'silos' of composer, genre, style, and place, as well as in many instances across the (notional) 1800 divide. All contributions appeal to a wide readership of scholars, students, practitioners and informed musical public.

Cambridge Elements ☰

Elements in Music and Musicians 1750–1850

Elements in the Series

Dr. Charles Burney and the Organ
Pierre Dubois

The Age of Musical Arrangements in Europe, 1780–1830
Nancy November

A full series listing is available at: www.cambridge.org/eimm

Printed in the United States
by Baker & Taylor Publisher Services